MW01672946

As the seasons pass us by,
So our lives in cycles spin
Like a merry-go-round, we're caught in the thrill
of the ride.
Unsure how we boarded and when it will end,
We shout as we reach for the golden ring:

LET'S GO AROUND AGAIN

A COLLECTION OF WRITINGS

BY

ELLEN K. WILLIAMS

Published by

CATTAIL PRESS
150 Baltusrol Road
Fairfield Glade, TN 38558

First Edition 2009
Copyright © 2009 by Ellen K. Williams
All rights reserved

ISBN 978-0-9672791-9-0

Library of Congress Control Number 2009932044

DEDICATIONS

To Joe, my husband, who has, for 45 years, listened to all of my verses, stories and essays, and continues to be my greatest source of inspiration.

To Christian McTurk, M.D., our son, who read and loved the originals and all of the revisions, and whose expression of pride has significantly contributed to my achievements.

To Christian's wife, Debby, and daughters Arya and Erica, whose comments I have treasured and whose loving support has been welcomed.

To my stepdaughter Liz O'Connor, her husband, Mike, and daughter, Calleigh, for their positive feedback.

To my stepdaughter Lori Bock, and her husband, Jack, for their interest and support.

To my sister, Bea Petersen; her daughter Cheryl and Cheryl's husband, Gordon Nichols, her daughter Linda Petersen; for Bea's patience and helpful comments and for the interest and positive words from all of her family.

A Special Dedication

For my sister Bea Petersen, who was born in Denmark, raised in the United States, and has lived mostly in Sweden, yet has always been my lifelong friend and constant loving role model. She has been and continues to be an honored treasure for her extended family. Mange Tak, Bea.

ACKNOWLEDGMENTS

For the support of three editors: Michael Northen of "Wordgathering," David Walker (1948 - 2009) and Dean Hutson of "Our Senior Times." For the expertise of Mary Greene, who edited and formatted, and author Paul Leighty, who assembled my collection of writings into a real live book, I offer my heartfelt gratitude.

TABLE OF CONTENTS

ESSAYS

VERSES

SHORT STORIES

A MATTER OF TASTE

I used to think of myself as a pretty good cook. Gourmet? Maybe. But I certainly had developed pretty good taste buds.

My mother was an excellent, straight-from-the-heart-of-Copenhagen cook. Had she been wealthy she would have been known as a "chef." Her salmon, meatballs, dill cream sauce, sweet and sour red cabbage were heavenly; as were her apple cake, jellied rhubarb with raspberries, Danish (of course) pastries and little decorated fruits known as marzipan. To accompany the evening meal were candlelight and fresh flowers from her garden. On special occasions an eight-course smorgasbord included an aperitif called Akaquavit and Danish beer. The abundance of food was similar to a renaissance feast, which typically lasted three to four hours, including eating, drinking, toasting and singing the old Danish songs. My mother was authentic. She was raised beside the sea in a land of butter, creamy thick sauces and seafood. The food she prepared was real and authentic. She ground the liver for her liver pâté and marinated the salmon and herring. I loved it, most of it anyway; lox never really impressed me.

So, what's this all about? Me, a first-generation American, speaking Danish and English since birth, finding myself in a strange land, otherwise known as Tennessee, having lived most of my life in New York State with pods of Danes in every direction. This place is strange and the food even more strange. When my husband and I first arrived here and would go out for breakfast, we could not help but notice the wait staff serving gobs of white stuff ladled on top of gobs of baked white dough, with some dark-colored lumps sticking out. It was called "biskits and gravee" and even though I had announced that I wanted to acclimate by eating the native foods and thereby educate myself, in part, to the ways of these peoples, I could not, most definitely not, even consider to sample the mounds of mush!

What happened next was slow and insidious, like all evil, creepy, lurking happenings. I developed a friendship with a native woman and would go to brunch with her and watch her relish her biscuits and gravy while I dined on my New York egg whites and dry rye toast. Finally, I lost my calm and composure and gave in to the voice in my ear that said, "Go ahead, one little bit won't hurt…try it!" The native woman lured me further by saying: "Just try a half-order to begin with to see if you like it." HAH!!! I was on to her!! How conniving can you be? Here I was, teetering on the edge of the abyss of obesity, breathing in the fats and carbs from the infamous "biskits and gravy," and I tried it—and It Was Love at First Bite!!

How the innocent have fallen! Now, when on the plateau of the Cumberland Mountains and we drop by a small roadside restaurant, I begin salivating at the thought of indulging in my love affair with a gentle mound of off-white creamy sauce, enhanced with nuggets of nurtured pork sausage, lovingly ladled, three or four times over flaky warm biscuits, seasoned lightly, like a first kiss. A feast for kings!

How to resolve this dilemma? How can I ever explain to my Scandinavian preference my new love of Southern Delights? Don't have to. The foods actually complement one another. At first I felt as if I was turning away from the "old country—Denmark" but not so. I've discovered that I can embrace strange ways, strange food and strange people, as my parents and immigrants before and after them did, and not feel threatened, but feel welcomed most of the time. That is not to say that I love ALL greens, pork hocks, butts and grits, but… I'm still learning… How about a marinated herring?

WAITING ROOM BLUES

When I walked into the doctor's waiting room, I had just finished breakfast. Later I enjoyed a lunch break, and now I'm thinking about where to eat dinner. I've lost track of time, no, not the minutes, but the months and year. I think, or believe, it's 2000 something, but I'm not going to ask 'cause they'll call out the men in white suits carrying butterfly nets. Not knowing the year is a dead giveaway to one of the questions testing a patient's sanity, e.g., "Is the patient oriented to time, person and place?" So, quickly I'll add: I know it's 2008, but orientation to "place" in a waiting room where there are no windows, eclectic furnishings and perpetual music becomes a challenge.

It's a nice office. I should know because I've had time to intimately get to know its contents and design. I was really appreciative of the many original works of art. I think it took me about one hour to study the various mediums and composition of the hangings, took me a half hour or so to locate the artist's name and phone number, then another 30 minutes to negotiate an agreeable sale price. The office receptionist assured my husband and me that we had plenty of time to celebrate our new acquisition during lunch with the artist.

Upon our return, the receptionist informed us that our 45-minute delay now put us at the end of the appointment list, even though they had approved our absence. I assumed that perhaps we had misunderstood and accepted the new plan of waiting by reading the latest *Popular Mechanics*, *Golf*

Lessons, No. 16 and browsing through the complete set of *Children's Biblical Stories*, since the more popular magazines diminish in number with each hour.

People in a waiting room seem to be a disgruntled sort. Most of them apparently could benefit from an attitude adjustment. They scowl at one another, gulp at their bottled water and engage in loud sighing, snorting plugged-up nostrils, coughing, hacking and heavy breathing, accompanied by long, noisy exhales of breath. Occasionally they may look at one another, glance at their watch, shake their head back and forth while making a "tisk" sound, done by quickly forcing one's tongue from the roof of the mouth to the floor of the mouth culminating in a loud clicking noise, all performed while rolling the eyes in a broad sweep across the ceiling, accompanied by one long, enormous expulsion of air.

In all fairness, not all docs are tardy and have a hard time keeping to a schedule. As unbelievable as it may sound, some (two in the entire world) are even timely. These two are my son (of course), and a doc I heard about in Anchorage, Alaska, who had to keep his patients moving lest they suffer from frostbite.

The moment finally arrives. The inner-sanctum door opens and, though I expect two medieval court musicians clothed in silken striped red and yellow balloon pants, blaring on trumpets decorated with purple and gold flags, a voice that would carry to the last row of a theater announces: "Jane Doe!" I jump out of my chair, 'cause already the doc's assistant looks irritated that I'm not traveling at warp speed. She warmly greets me with, "Turn right first door on the left." Did I really say "Thank you"? Probably so, because my white-coat syndrome has set in and is interfering with whatever remembrance I had of why I am here!!

We now enter Waiting Room #2, otherwise known as "The Final Answer," or "This is it—the Really Big One," or "Now After All These Weeks of Feeling Punk, I'm Finally Going to Find Out What's Going to Kill Me Probably in Three Days and Better Get My Affairs in Order." Before leaving for room #2, and before your name is called, you had best collect your favorite stash of magazines (while there are still some left), or you'll be sequestered in the inner room with nothing to look at except colorful enlarged posters of the colon, kidney, lungs and miscellaneous organs, diseased or otherwise.

When you've finally arrived in the inner room, it is in this room you pull out your notes to remind yourself of your various ailments, and when the doc's assistant enters and in a real friendly-like manner says, "Well, what's your problem?" you refer to your list of medical complaints and discover you are nervously reciting your grocery list.

Seriously, being an advocate of assuming some responsibility for one's own well-being, at the beginning of my annual physical, I produced a 2"x3" card listing my health concerns. Horrified, the physician took his copy, and as his voice rose an entire octave, said "My god, what is this? I can't get to all of this!"

What's a patient to do? Multiple Choice—choose any three:

Learn and practice self-hypnosis and other relaxation techniques.

Take several books with you to your appointment, such as: *War and Peace* and *Rise and Fall of the Roman Empire*.

Bring your favorite pillow with you and take a long nap.

Practice your conversational and social skills with other patients.

Bring a deck of cards and board games.

As a last resort, sing "The Waiting Room Blues."

(ALL TOGETHER NOW—in blues style)

We got the waiting room blues
And that's no lie.
We wait and we snooze
And in between we cry
'cause we haven't seen the wife
or the kiddies all day,
and if I value my life
I better get going right away.

We got the W. R. Blues
Just hear what we say,
The W. R. Blues
Just won't go away.
Yea, yea, yea.

YOU'RE TO BLAME, MR. PIERPOINT

There are some things I just don't understand about the holidays. Since we were kids, we sang the usual holiday songs, but remember how often you never really understood the meaning of the carol? I imagine that some of us, now of grown-up status, still don't. For instance, did you ever stop to think about a song entitled "Jingle Bells"? What does it really mean?

It was written in 1857 by James Pierpoint for a Thanksgiving holiday, and for some reason was never used until the Christmas celebrations, which is really too bad, as we have a plethora of Yuletide songs and a sparse collection of Thanksgiving tunes. Oh, well, let's stay in the holiday spirit and have some fun with Mr. Pierpoint's song. (Hmmm, I wonder if it would have made a better Thanksgiving song.)

"Jingle bells, jingle bells, jingle all the way." The song has a total of two stanzas and three verses. The three verses contain the word "jingle" eighteen times, probably one of the reasons kids love to sing it. You don't have to know all the lyrics, and if you forget them, you can just stand there and mumble "jingle bells" over and over and over, and...

I thought bells clanged, ding-donged, rang out, gonged, or even peeled across the hills and valleys, but a thin, shallow little jingle does sound somewhat insipid, meek and inconsequential! Shouldn't a bell ring out across the land in majestic tenor, announcing noble coronations, events of worth and substance and glory!? Oh, well, perhaps a weak jingle is better than none. We're told the bells "jingle all the way." Which way? How far is all the way?

No one has even informed us where we are or where we're headed.

The next line of the song is thoroughly and purely presumptive: "Oh, what fun it is to ride in a one-horse open sleigh!" Good grief!! Does that really presume; no, it *states*, that in the midst of winter, it is fun to huddle in an open sleigh, with no protection from the harsh winds whipping about our faces, traveling at a rather slow speed (since we have only one horse), shivering, quivering—and it's fun? No, it is not fun! It is agony. It is miserable, and the bells are driving us crazy, and we're freezing.

This may sound like a silly question, especially since the deed is done, but couldn't we have obtained a closed-in carriage, or a sleigh with a roof and doors? Maybe it would have been referred to as "a one-horse closed-in sleigh"?

Sadly and regrettably, the yuletide song continues: "Dashing through the snow, in a one-horse open sleigh, o'er the fields we go, laughing all the way." You say they're laughing? My dear sir, that's probably simple hysteria you're hearing, begging for disembarkation, nourishment and warmth. They're crying, Mr. Pierpoint, crying. I would be too, if I were in an open, one-horse buggy. Doesn't it seem a tad unreasonable, why, whoever was in charge of this questionable outing, couldn't have hired two horses so we could get to wherever it is we don't know where we're going faster?

Who is "Miss Fannie Bright"? James (the composer), in the second stanza, says when he thought he'd take a ride, this Fanny person showed up at his side! Without ascribing fault, he tells us they wound up in a snow bank. Well, prudence dictates we avoid drawing hasty conclusions and only hope they weren't hurt, and apparently they were not, because they immediately resumed singing "Jingle Bells…," etc.

Let's see, we left the song with "Bells on bobtails ring, making spirits bright." Do you really believe that your spirits are going to brighten whenever the bells jingle? If frostbite has not taken hold, a sip or two of a hot toddy might possibly lift your spirits. This was easily done, according to the tune "Here we come a Wassailing," by surrounding the entrance door to a well-appointed home and loudly singing the wassailing carol. Hopefully, the carolers' efforts were rewarded by a cup of punch from the "Wassail Bowl." Such a practice was labeled as "caroling" or "wassailing" and is popular to the present day. If the singing was not too frightful, perhaps an invitation was extended to enjoy a second cup from the wassail bowl inside the cozy house.

As we finally head for home, we are cautioned to be aware of numerous sightings of a small, chubby, elderly little fellow, white hair and beard, dressed in red (isn't that a bit obvious?) and creeping about surreptitiously, late at night, entering and leaving peoples' homes, by way of their chimneys! What is most peculiar is that he seems to bring huge bags of contraband in as well as out. I'm even told that he arrives and leaves in an open sleigh, and that his sleigh travels directly up into the sky, pulled by eight reindeer who fly!! My, the yuletide spirit certainly brings out the fun and the fanciful.

Well, Mr. Pierpoint, just wanted to send a little greeting your way. Don't take my venting too seriously, 'cause as simple as your little ditty is, it certainly seems to have survived over the years and should it be sung at Thanksgiving instead of Christmas (as originally intended), one could just sing "gobble gobble gobble all the way"—eighteen times.

WISHING YOU AND YOURS A JINGLE BELL HOLIDAY!

LOOKING AT THE MOON

I don't really remember when I first became confused about the moon. It used to be such a simple thing. It wasn't complicated. It had always been reliable, dependable, and if you counted correctly, you could depend upon it to be there, weather permitting, when you wanted to set the scene for a special relationship. For folks of a different generation, a "special relationship" involved couples who used to "spoon" (by the light of the silvery moon), "pitch woo," "make out" or "neck." Translated, the aforementioned phrases were used to describe affectionate gestures shared between two people. There was a certain amount of time devoted to the expression of their feelings for each other. People always became romantic under the light of the moon or because of the moon. Any size moon would do, but a full one offered the most promise and inspiration. According to current movies, television and literature, an expression of attraction to the opposite sex today might consist of "Hi, my name is John, what's yours, let's get a room," —and that is what happened to the moon.

With the event of moon exploration, we look at the moon differently, and it is no longer associated with love tunes, spoon and June, but with rockets, take-off and zero gravity. Moon-gazing is no longer a relaxing experience and "count down" assumes an entirely different meaning. The moon has changed its "face." What was once a spectacle of beauty and inspiration to poets from Shakespeare to T. S. Eliot has become a clump of matter awaiting instantaneous dissection and analysis for practical application. Do you suppose our hurried demands of assault and bombardment upon the moon (3-2-1-FIRE) have anything to do with our hurried demands of assault and bombardment upon each other?

It must have taken a few eons or so of trying to identify a white orb of changing shapes, hanging low, or sometimes high, in a black sky. After all, it gave no hints of its purpose, and ages of speculation produced no plausible explanation. It was probably long ago that a prehistoric female tried explaining her puzzling and unexplainable pregnancy by pointing up at the strange and seemingly inconstant object in the sky and saying: "chunga-chunga-wom-wom-bo." Meaning, it did it and not your cousin, and thereafter, the moon was honored for its fertile (or romantic) powers. (It has been suggested in some circles that women are still using the moon to explain their behaviors.)

Where is the day-dreamer, head-over-heels young love, old love and pure senseless romantic love that once thrived "under the light of the moon"? Now that we have trampled haphazardly with clumsy, heavy boots (or "moon" boots) on the surface of the moon, the thud that was heard throughout the universe and beyond (well, at least back on Earth) could have been the first step that may have spelled doom to the fairy tale, gossamer approach of enjoying the moon. Remember the cat and the fiddle with, of all things, a cow jumping over the moon, and, how about an owl and a pussycat married by a turkey, dining on mince and slices of quince and then all of them dancing by the light of the MOON. Not by the light of the sun or the stars—and to be sure we understood, the author repeats it twice: "They danced by the light of the moon, The moon, The moon."!!! The poem first appeared in the right side of the author's brain, the creative side, not the science side, but the right side. If we stopped using the right side of our brain, would it shrivel up and no longer deliver silly stuff like animals getting married—or colors or starlight or moonglow? Would the moon just become a useful tool for scientific pursuits? Would it still take my breath away during one of its more outstanding presentations?

Our behaviors towards the moon have been erratic. At one time, before our journeys into space, we looked at the moon differently, and we poetically dissected it, sang to it, danced to it, howled, shrieked, cursed and moaned at it and offered performances of all sorts of physical gyrations, native dances, dances of good and evil, witch dances, and various supine positions indicating our previous inferior place in the cosmic arena. Inferior, because in the heyday of moon dances, we hadn't visited the moon yet. Following that accomplishment, the popularity of moon worship dances hit an all time low. There followed yet another phase when we were absolutely senseless, loony, illogical and downright stupid-sounding when it came to our satellite. It seems we began to believe the powers and special meanings we attributed to the moon. From the drawings of cave men, writers of poems, novels, essays, plays, song writers, theater or movies, we frequently referred to the moon and its mystic powers. Creative artists attached supernatural meaning to the moon, and why shouldn't it be so? Folklore affixes tales of lunacy relating to the belief that many of us have a tendency towards emotional imbalance during certain phases of the moon. (Incredibly, there is a theory of unknown origin that suggests the imbalance occurs primarily with the female gender. However, there is mounting evidence that the infirmity is being transferred to the male gender as well and at a rapid pace.) Gypsy folklore explained that werewolves changed into their animal component whenever the moon was full, and they prowled in reaction to the moon and ocean tides. During the times when myths and folklore were popular, a social hostess needed to be quite attentive to the phase of the moon when compiling her guest list, should she inadvertently serve a spontaneous metamorphosis for dessert.

Long before rockets for space, there were wagons for hayrides under a harvest moon sky, back porch swings (is there such a thing anymore?) for swinging under the light of the moon, and moonlit ice-skating rinks in the park, all accompanied by moon music. Some were absurd and silly musical attempts to serenade your sweetie, while others such as Beethoven's "Moonlight Sonata" and Debussy's "Au Claire de Lune" were rendered from the masters. The 30's and 40's seemed to have no end of moon tunes. To name but a few: "Moonlight in Vermont," "By the light of the Silvery Moon," "Blue Moon," "Moonglow," "Full Moon and Empty Arms" (taken from Rachmaninoff's Piano Concerto No. 2), "Harvest Moon" and saving the worst until last, "When the Moon Hits Your Eye Like a Big Pizza Pie, That's Amore." (If it is, heaven help us!)

Where did the moon music go? Many of the songs of the past had real staying power, but when was the last song written about the moon? What if there will never be another one? If not, to whom or to what would we croon or lament? "Melody of Mars?," "The Jupiter Jump?," "Saturn serenade"?

Fortunately, moon music is still around, though not to the extent as in previous decades.

You may think this entire matter trivia, but imagine if we no longer pined for the moon, if there was no moon? What would we call someone who is moonstruck, if not moonstruck? Starstruck? Sunstruck? Just doesn't sound right.

Of even greater concern, there has been a "Man in the Moon" all my life, for as long as I can remember. What if such a phrase is deleted, wiped out? There is a scientific explanation that states the dark pockmarks suggest where the moon was struck by an asteroid early in its history. Now that sounds reasonable, but we prefer to cling to an old poem written years ago in Scotland by a youngster describing what she saw when she looked at the moon. At least the concept of the "Man in the Moon" makes more sense than, according to an old wives' tale, the moon is made of cream cheese.

In defense of the "Man in the Moon" theory, perhaps that's what we need; more childlike naiveté and less science. Our discovery of the moon's material composition and classification of same has not enhanced our appreciation of its beauty and magnificence shimmering upon a placid lake. However, inquisitive minds and scientific advances have led us to where we should be: exploring our planet and the space beyond. I imagine the National Aeronautics and Space Administration (NASA) and a good part of our population say tremendous advances have been made since our first moonstep for mankind. There are those who disagree. I think herein lies the confusion: Whom do you believe?

Reminds me of the story of *The Emperor's New Suit*, by Hans Christian Andersen. It seems the emperor needed a new suit and engaged the services of two tailors who, unknown to the emperor, were actually swindlers. The tailors dipped into their bag of (supposed) embroidered golden garments, and spread them out for the emperor to admire. The emperor looked and saw nothing, but not wanting to appear unknowledgeable of fine materials, praised the tailors' choices.

The day arrived when the tailors delivered his fine suit to the emperor. The emperor put the suit on (or so he pretended), his loyal servants held up the long train (or so they imagined), and he then paraded through the streets so his citizens could admire and compliment his fine suit. His townspeople cheered the "golden garment" and applauded as he strode by. Toward the final steps of the parade stood a mother holding her small child, who loudly proclaimed, "But he has nothing on at all."

Have we reached a point where we must face the naked truth and stop pretending that we have achieved notable and significant strides in space and lunar exploration? There is little doubt that we have acquired progress in the scientific community because of our moon investigations, but has the pendulum swung too far and for too long?

Have we silenced our senses, dimmed the celestial music and become no longer even aware of whether tonight's moon is full, new, waxing or waning?

When was the last time you looked at the moon?

Do you recall the sight of an ascending orange moon so full it's about to burst and spill over the horizon?

Did you ever see a sliver of a new moon, a crescent in a blue-gray sky with the evening star twinkling at its tip?

Remember a stark white globe in a black sky leaving a white pathway on black waters?

Have you seen towering black pine trees stretching towards the moon, their tips yearning to touch the transient orb?

Have you heard the night music of the owl and the whippoorwill trying to convince the moon to stay and not dance away with the dawn?

Have you seen black clouds drift by the front of the moon, envying those clouds in the full light behind the moon, and smaller clouds, on both sides of the moon, completing the heavenly canvas?

It could be that now is the time for us to change our orientation and just swing on the back porch glider with someone we like and quietly gaze at the moon, the moon, the moon.

I SHOT THE RADIO IN THE WOMEN'S LOCKER ROOM

I did.

I was showering after my workout, to the incessant accompaniment of what is commonly referred to as rock or hop-along "music." I've heard it many times before, but this time the "music" sounded as if someone was suffering under torture, screaming up high, moaning down low, and crying in agony. I felt so sorry for those poor singers (I guess that's what they were called) and desperately wanted to help them. I quickly threw on some clothes, pulled out my air-soft plastic pellet BB gun, (softest type of air-soft gun available, mainly used for shooting backyard varmints or general hunting), ran down the hallway of the locker room, shouted "hit the deck" to the ladies holding their hair dryers up in the air and looking aghast at me; took aim at the speaker screen on the ceiling that was blasting forth all that noise, pulled the trigger and, fortunately, as the radio screen was made of plastic, it cracked into pieces and the sound went: ARG- R –G ---E-EK-UH... Silence.

Oh, heavenly day. Silence. Pure silence. Oh, oh, wait. What's that high-pitched siren? Could that be the police? I think I hear a ruckus at the front door, the locker room door barges open, and a man wearing a police uniform is shouting, "OK, ladies, don't move, drop your dryers and put up your hands!"

"It's not us," one of the ladies shouted. "It's her," she exclaimed, pointing at me. "She went bananas!"

"OK, missy crazy lady, drop that dryer, uh, gun, on the floor and put your hands up!"

"But officer, I didn't do anything, really. It's the music, the music, that's it, that's what driving me crazy. I hear it wherever I go, in the grocery store, the department stores, the dentist's office, the doc's office; I'll probably even hear it in the funeral home—for my funeral!! Oh, my.

"All right lady, that's enough. You better come with me and take a little ride downtown."

"Oh, officer, I'll be all right, I swear I will be. I promise never to fire another BB gun again."

"Listen, lady, you're gonna hafta put up with that music stuff called, "rock" or "hophip" or whatever it's called. All the rest of us do, why can't you? In fact, you come with me to the paddy wagon, I'll take you to the station and sign you up for classes, desensitization classes, and so whenever you hear that kind of music, you'll love it!"

"No, I don't want to go into your little wagon or whatever you call it, and I don't want any classes. Besides, how could that possibly work?!"

The officer explained, "Well, you sit at a desk, and you've got a lot of buttons in front of you that are marked 'Mozart,' 'Beethoven,' 'Bach,' 'Guy Lombardo,' 'Al Jolson,' and so on, and when you press one of those buttons you get to hear a little of that music followed by a very low-voltage electric shock. To stop the shock, you press one of the other buttons marked 'Suburban Voodoo' or 'KISS' or 'I'm with Stupid.'

"See, it's easy and won't really hurt at all."

"Then you mean, I'll never hear my favorite music again?"

"Don't worry, lady, you won't even want to!"

"Martha, Martha, wake up, Martha!!" Alfred took Martha's hand and shook it gently. Martha opened her eyes.

"Alfred, you better get rid of that gun we bought, and I'm never going to that gym again. Why, they take people away in little wagons, and they never come back as the same person they were when they left!!"

"Now, now, Martha, you were having a bad dream, that's all. Better wake up now though, it's time to get ready for the symphony concert."

"Oh, good, are they playing 'Rock and Roll All Nite' by KISS?"

TO PASS OR NOT TO PASS

The year is 1850. You have a barn to raise or some bottomland that needs help with the plowing. The men will bring their tools, and the ladies will bring the food, which will be placed in the shade and later enjoyed when the hot sun finally goes down. Everyone will celebrate the results of their combined efforts and, as the sun sets, will enjoy the food everyone brought "to pass."

"To pass" really means "so as to lighten the load for all and not overwhelm the hostess, or the cook of the house."

Folks understood the nature of the event and would search in their larders for plain, but tasty meats or fruit and fresh vegetables from the garden. As typical of those days, concerns always had to be given to the matter of keeping foods cold since refrigeration was not to see its beginnings until some twenty years hence with the onset of the "ice box." If half of us got the "runs" later that day, and the next day some keel over, that's to be expected. Life spans are short and ole Doc Brown lives too far away to accurately diagnose what ails us. Botulism or death by mayo was probably common, but referred to as "a bug" or "he's been ailing."

In our present century, most barns are no longer "raised" with the help of our neighbors, nor are acres plowed with the help of our sturdy oxen, but we still follow a tradition of "bringing a dish to pass." With a little stretch of the imagination, let's revisit this style of communal feasting and decide: Will you bring a dish to pass, or will you pass by a dish, or will you just help yourself to the dish you brought?

We arrive at the home of the brave hostess (every hostess is brave or has an overload of feel-good chemicals, either naturally or synthetically, that must account for his/her willingness to play waiter/waitress, chef, housekeeper maître d, and bartender).

Now, there's that cute young bride. She still has a honeymoon glow in her eyes while she tells us about her wedding gifts, including a chef's knife, that she uses for "just everything. I line up the raw chicken, the vegetables and chop them without even stopping to rinse it off. What a time saver! It would have taken me twice as long if I had to wash it off all the time." Hopefully, she'll acquire a friend or relative who will mention the need to wash knives while using them.

The buffet table is a groaning board of every sort of "feel good" and "yummy" food you can imagine, but do you have any idea what you're scooping onto your plate? Chances are good that you don't know. Most of the entrees have no label identifying the contents, and I usually like to know what I'm eating. It must be difficult for the cooks and the hostess to meet the demands of persons with special diets, and a tip of the hat goes to those who take the time to make labels and even provide a 3"x5" card with the recipe of the treasured dish they made for the occasion. The cards sound like extra work in addition to the cooking, plus I'm not sure I could translate "a little bit of this" and "a pinch of that" into definable terms that others would understand. The lack of label, however, has a distinct advantage. If no one likes your contribution, just pretend ignorance and act as though you never saw it before in your life. Disown it! In order to successfully achieve this and not involve your favorite serving dish, deliver your casserole in a plastic throw-away dish. No labels also suit dishes that allow you to get rid of leftovers. You just chop, sort and sauce, and if you label it, give it an exotic name like Mexicali Svengalali ChaCha!

Dishes that may cause some concern are those that are plugged in, kept warm on a low setting, have contents that look gray, tan, or brown with black lumps that are bubbling slowly, very slowly. One bubble gets fatter, plops open, audibly hissssses and fizzzzes, then stealthily disperses and tunnels to the underground below, making a path for the next bubble to follow. If entertainment is low on your list, folks could always watch for the next bubble to plop.

One buffet table looked rather non-threatening until suddenly, I noticed several mean-looking casseroles, and as I was reaching across them, something grabbed me around the forearm; twisting and tightening and wiggling until I reached over and grabbed it, and in my blind fury, ripped it off and slammed it across the table where it splashed into a dipping bowl of white gloopy stuff. Victorious! I smirked at my assailant—ha-ha! I… got you!... you… you… stalk of, er… er… celery? Well, it did have a pretty tight grip, and you never know…

Colorful bowls, and brightly-painted dishes, especially those with floral patterns, always enhance the visual effects of the line of serving dishes. Once, toward the end of the evening, I just had to look at the bottom of an almost empty, simply gorgeous bowl used for serving the potato salad, to learn of its origin and it read: "Made in Yucatan, toxic materials, not to be used with food." Whoops.

Hosting a dish-to-pass party is not necessarily easier than doing all of your own cooking. The hostess usually needs to assign food items so as to avoid duplication, and she will also bake a ham or roast a turkey as her offering. And, when the entrees arrive, she'll need to orchestrate their position and place, plug them in, wrap them up, freeze them, chill them, warm them or boil them, etc.

As the guests are preparing to leave, the hostess may be found slicing and assembling little take-home packages for each person or couple. I recall one lady, who usually arrived late, brought no casserole, but did bring her own large plastic containers for the hostess to fill for that lady's family dinner the next day.

Ok, so this sounds like an exaggeration. Certainly, buffets can work out well, if you enjoy taking chances. But I really felt empathy for my friend who, once the guests had left, knocked upon my door, looking frazzled, distressed and mumbling to herself, loaded down with white plastic bags labeled with white tags, trying to return the empty and washed dishes to those folks who say, "Oh, never mind washing it now, I'll pick it up later or whenever..." She scoops to the bottom of one bag, saying, "I know your dish is in here somewhere. Oh, heavens, gotta hurry before it gets too dark. Here, is this yours? No? Well, take it anyway, it looks pretty good. Gotta run, see ya..."

The alternative of providing your own buffet is not so bad. Invite your friends, call your favorite take-out place and pick up the order. Also, there are usually several nearby caterers of sound reputation who will provide (and deliver) at a reasonable charge, whatever you desire. I know, it lacks the homey touch—and what will happen to your reputation as the best cook on the block—and what will people think? They might just think, "Oh, how nice. I received a dinner invitation, and I don't have to cook."

There are those who might say that I'm making a moot point, because it will no longer be a problem, whether or not I choose to attend a dinner where I would contribute, because once my friends have read this article, I have probably received my last invitation that includes a dish to pass, or not to pass, or any other way you can possibly imagine.

Bon Appetit!
No Gratuity Expected.

SALLY AND MAGGIE

"Dearest Maggie, you're going to be just fine," Sally said. "Everyone has had surgery, well, mostly everyone. There's really nothing to worry about. Whether it's elective or selective, just tell yourself you can do it. The body believes every word the mind tells it, you know. You just have to make sure you've got all your ducks in a row."

"I know, I know," Maggie said, "but why in the world are you talking about ducks? I mean I'm…"

"Scared, right?" interrupted Sally. "Everyone feels that way. Even if it's just for a hangnail, it's all serious and scary. As they say, there's no such thing as minor surgery. I would call that an oxymoron, wouldn't you?"

"I guess; however, I'm not a moron," interrupted Maggie. "I have enough sense to realize that if I keep busy, it will help to keep my mind off of it. But you have no idea what that doctor said. He's the one who's doing the female surgery, you know, 'down there.' I think they call it a hammock or a sling, or something like that, but let me tell you what he said. I was *so* upset."

"What do you mean?" asked Sally.

"Well, the nurse had taken my history, and I told her, along with all the other medical details, that I had PD. She asked how long and if it had spread to anyone else. I told her certainly not, and I believe I manage it rather well through exercise, diet and medication. Well, here I am on the exam table, and while the doc was checking me out, he asked the date of my last bout of venereal disease. 'Venereal disease!' I shouted. 'I do *not* have venereal disease! I have Parkinson's Disease ~ PD! NOT VD!!' I was so taken aback that I bolted forward to a sitting position, bumped right into him and sent him flying backwards, half-way across the room, on his little round stool on wheels. While helping him up, the nurse apologized for her mistake and said she didn't hear me clearly. Huh! I guess not.

"Later, in his office, he said I was a suitable candidate for his surgery, which is a good thing since it's scheduled for next week, and he recommended that I have my internist check me out, partly routine and partly because of my Parkinson's.

"Now, it appears I'm not such a suitable candidate after all. My internist wants a cardiologist to check me over because of some symptoms I reported, and it might include some sort of heart test where they put a tube in an artery. He also said he was canceling my female surgery.

"OK, I almost went ballistic because I had really taken some time to prepare my wardrobe, laying out just the right outfits, matching shoes and scarves and special facial makeup including just the right shade of powder..." (here, Maggie paused to catch her breath, having worked herself into a state of frustration, took a deep breath and continued on), "to offset those glaring hospital ceiling lights, and worst of all, I'm not even sure if I'll need those outfits because the heart test is usually not an overnight stay."

Exasperated by now, Maggie, speaking to herself, said "OK, OK, adjust, adjust; put things in order of their importance, and get busy and juggle all these doc appointments so I can fit in my lunches and club meetings."

"Really, Maggie, what's more important, your medical condition or your appearance?" Sally asked.

"What's the difference? Every time I turn around something else is wrong with me. You talked about ducks in a row; well, how about the feeling that all the docs are playing 'Round Robin' with me—just going from one to another. Ducks and robins indeed! There had better not be some old bird waiting his turn in line."

"Hah! That's better," laughed Sally. Sounds as though you may be getting your sense of humor back."

"Well, the following doesn't exactly tickle my fancy. My internist is making an appointment for me with the cardiologist, which certainly couldn't have been the next day because that's when I had an appointment with my eye doc for yet another exam. Let's see, don't find anything too funny there." Continuing on, Maggie explained, "The eye doc gave me a prescription for new glasses, although he said I would probably want cataract surgery soon. I told him I will delay the eye fix until I find out if I need a heart test, and also until I can find out about the date of surgery for the other end. Can you guess what he said then?"

"Sure," Sally said jokingly, "he said to wait until you know which end is up!!"

"Oh, now stop. He agreed it would be best not to fill that eye prescription until after the heart test, and I know I must have done a slack jaw, 'cause I said, "You mean because I might not make it through the test?"

"He replied, 'Of course not, but maybe by then you won't have such a full plate,'" Maggie explained.

"Can you imagine, Sally, I'm on such a starvation diet now that my plate has forgotten how to be full. Ha ha," joked Maggie.

"And if it ever did get too full, you'd just get a doggie bag," quipped Sally.

"Say, since we're being so silly," giggled Sally, "have you ever heard that some doctors sing while they're doing surgery?"

"Oh, sure," Maggie replied, "and they probably sing something like this:

'Gimme some Ole Black Magic,
Might Just do the trick,

Unless you think of something else real quick
'Cause every time your eyes meet mine, I
think
Oh, oh, she didn't get enough anesthesia!!'"

"Oh, you're kidding, that's so funny," Sally laughed. "And I suppose the patients sing "All of Me."

And now, both singing: "Why not take all of us? Can't you see, of us there's too darn much?"

"OK, enough!" pleads Maggie. "I have more scheduling to do."

"In heaven's name, what more could there possibly be... bad liver? flat feet? too much hot air?" (giggling) "But we've always known that!"

Ignoring Sally's comments, Maggie explained, "I had scheduled a sitting for a portrait of myself at a well-known studio as a gift for our granddaughters. Now, I can't possibly do a flattering picture because worrying about pending surgery might give me frown marks. However, the photographer assured me he could do wonders with touch-up paint. I told him I didn't know if there was enough touch-up paint in the world for a woman my age," giggled Maggie. "Of course, I was only kidding."

Sally replied, "Well, I've found the solution. Whenever I see someone nearby with a camera, I immediately cradle my chin in my hands, with my elbows propped up on a table and then sneak my thumbs under my jaw and chin and very carefully pull back some of the loose skin and, just ever so slightly, smile. Try it, it really works. But I do agree, photographers can do miracles these days, even on gals like us."

"Miracles?? Well!!" Maggie responded, "but, there's one more thing I haven't told you, and it's my most important concern of all. I went to a lot of trouble getting a pedicure so my feet would look good on the operating table. Those docs and nurses notice things like that. Deciding what color polish to put on your toenails is no easy feat. (Whoops, didn't mean the pun). I couldn't decide between Midnight Orchid or Raspberries and Cream, so I went with Glowing Peach. What do you think?" asked Maggie.

"I think you concentrate on your appearance as a way of avoiding or not accepting your medical problems... or were you talking about the pedicure, color-wise?" Sally responded.

"I was talking about the color of my toenails and not your kitchen-sink psychology, and if the docs insist upon some heart test, how in the world am I going to work in another pedicure? You know those pedicurists require plenty of advance notice."

"So, in other words, Maggie, you're saying:

'If your feet aren't pretty on the operating table
With your toes painted red and looking real smart
Might as well postpone on fixin' up the heart
To a day when the toes can be looking their best,
Should they go out the door ahead of all of the rest.'"

"Oh, Sally, I was just teasing. You know I don't mean that. This says it all:

'One doc, two docs, three in a row
One for the body, and one for the cardio,
One for the eyes, one more for the cysto,
All together now, around and 'round we go
SWING YOUR PARTNERS AND DOSEY DOE!'"

A SECOND LOOK AT THE FIRST THANKSGIVING

History tells us that in 1621, at the Plymouth Plantation, in Plymouth, Massachusetts, about one hundred and fifty persons, consisting of native tribal people and colonists, organized and attended a feast-of-plenty known as The First Thanksgiving.

There are a few theories why they did this, namely, the Pilgrims wanted to meet some people with whom they had not shared close quarters on their voyage from England, and the native tribal people (later to be known as "Indians") were really the only nearby inhabitants to invite. It could also be that one of the more dominant ladies from England was eager to get a head start on the social ladder of success.

Feeding 150 persons is really a giant leap up the social ladder. The most common explanation for the invitation was to give a pat on the back to others and yourself for making it through the harvest and to bolster one another for the coming winter... but a celebration lasting for three days? The literature describes three days of feasting, though it seems that a hearty whack on the back and "job well done" or "whampa whampa ungo" (in Indian-speak) would have delivered the same sentiments.

It really is a wonder that the occasion wasn't later referred to as the "Thanksgiving Trials." It's hard to imagine two social groups with more differences and diverse customs than those of the Indians and the Pilgrims. To expect those early pioneers to wine and dine for three days, consuming food with a high potential of being rancid, if not just a trifle spoiled, and not suffer even a little indigestion that would most likely be blamed upon the visitor or the guest, (whichever one was which) is indeed fraught with the greatest of unrealistic expectation. Perhaps the designated party planners were a bit optimistic and ambitious; however, it appears that any mishaps or arguments were not reported either by smoke signals or by horse or mule, and because of the time it takes a normal delivery (sorry, no overnight deliveries) to go through, the news becomes rather stale, boring, lost or outdated.

I would have been most interested to see how they addressed their respective deities during Grace. The Indians most likely dozed off during the sermons by the Pilgrims, but imagine the colonists' reaction to worship by smoke, chants and unusual songs with explicit dances. In any event, the dinner promised to be a terrific way to break the ice and attempt to reduce any social stress.

Most written accounts and paintings of the feast depict a setting of about 20 natives and Pilgrims, seated at a rectangular table, pleasantly smiling and relaxed. Now, try to see that setting with 150 diners seated at many tables. Seating arrangements could be quite difficult. If a guest sat downwind from a native with four-week-old goose grease on his hair, there might be a hassle for an upwind seat, as with the neighbor of a Pilgrim who had not yet streamlined his use of the showers or laundry facilities.

The feast was a gastronomical challenge! As there was no refrigeration, one could only hope that the chefs were adept at preserving all the meats, fowl and fish.

Many wooden, store-bought (or traded) teeth lost the battle with some of the brittle, cured meats. Thorough cooking could always be assured with a fire and a spit, and smoked duck was a sought-after delicacy; however, you might take special care if you're thinking of reaching across your neighbor to stab a piece that caught your eye, since there were no forks, and a knife might send the wrong message. The remaining utensils in use were spoons and your hands, while one's sleeve served as a handy napkin.

The menu on that day in 1621 most likely included plain vegetables, some fruits, but not apples. There was no corn on the cob, mashed potatoes, bread stuffing or pumpkin pie. Those particular foods had not yet been cultivated, were unknown to that particular region, and there was no refrigeration to maintain freshness. Fowl such as wild turkey, ducks, and geese, as well as main courses of venison and fish, were plentiful. A dessert might have been unsweetened cranberries.

Unfortunately, and with regard to the years that followed, the foods in the first Thanksgiving feast gradually took on an altogether different, almost unrecognizable and bizarre appearance. We gradually started slip-sliding along on a downhill greasy path... of lard, of fat, of cream, of butter... The slim, trim turkey became a greasy "butterball," not only injected with butter upon slaughtering, but butter was slathered on copiously during its cooking stage as well. Our salivary glands must have changed significantly and begun to demand more attention, because eventually it became necessary to prep the turkey for a cooking magazine photo-shoot by applying tan-colored shoe polish on the skin, presumably to inspire us to prepare a similar abomination. The simple potato was cooked, pulverized and engulfed in butter and cream, along with a bread stuffing consisting more of pork sausage than bread, and our vegetables were cubed, mashed, fried, sauced and mutilated beyond recognition. Similarly, the simple pumpkin was smashed to smithereens, and countless desserts were buried under mounds of sugar and salt—and just for good measure, more salt.

We plead guilty for our preference for the roly-poly plump November holiday dinner and rationalize our consumption by saying, “Oh, well, it only happens once a year.” What “only happens once a year”? The holiday or our on-going hearty consumption spelled with a capital “D” for disaster, as in the current disaster epidemic of diabetes, increased heart attacks and strokes?

So, where does all this take us? It takes us in a full circle right back to the beginning of that famous first Thanksgiving dinner, preparing and eating food the way it should be eaten, prepared so it’s closer to the original source and not so far removed that it is no longer identifiable—and consisting of plain turkey, pure vegetables and fruits, fish, some game and fowl and a dessert of plain unsweetened cranberries.

Seconds, anyone?

MASQUERADE

Want to know the truth? I really don't want to write about the disease I have, but it appears as though my choices are limited since the two, the disease and the writing, are inseparable and strange bedfellows. Writing about it will not make the disease disappear, decrease or ease the related frustration, impatience or anger. The feelings inside will not diminish any more than the pasted-on smile that I wear, will cover them. I am not a heroine who plows ahead through scheduled exercises, weight machines and pool exercises just so I won't walk worse tomorrow. I cough, drool and tremble, speak too softly and have almost reinvented myself to become someone I'm desperately trying to camouflage. I want you to know me as I once was and not as I probably am now. "Probably," because I'm not sure myself what the new and unimproved me is and/or has become. Moreover, I will not allow you to know the many "me's." Many, because I wear different disguises to fool you, but mainly to fool me. My disguises are my stories, my poems, my essays or any literary form that will suit my subject of expression.

I was told that I "probably" had Parkinson's Disease approximately 5-6 years ago. It started with slowness throughout one side of my body, not rendering me severely disabled, just slower. I refused to accept the diagnosis, even though I eventually began taking meds to replace the diminishing dopamine from the brain. My anger was joined by depression and inactivity, leading eventually to an office visit with a psychotherapist, who challenged me to write about my effect, my feelings. Writing about feelings does not necessarily mean ownership of the feelings. I'm capable of writing in quite an abstract fashion and from a rather remote distance. I had to show how much of a superwoman I was. Not only was I capable of having a progressive, non-curable disease of the brain, but I would be able to handle it better than anyone else. I refused to complain about my discomfort and certainly would avoid asking for or receiving help.

Moreover, sympathy was not acceptable from whomever or whenever, nor would I degrade myself by wallowing in self-pity. The rendering of pity by a well-meaning friend has only one interpretation for the receiver: I am less capable than you.

And so I wrote. Even though I had written a smattering of poems years ago, and had studied literature, I was astonished that the ability had not only lingered on but had flourished while asleep. I wrote about anger, and initially, it was my own, my anger, but then I learned how to wear all kinds of disguises and learned how to assign the anger or whatever the effect, to an inanimate object—a hat, for example—that wore the grief and anguish for me. It belonged to that hat, for instance, and was experienced by the hat, and not by me.

Other guises came quickly, and I became a painter of nature using words as my medium, without oils, pastels, or watercolors, I painted images behind which I found refuge and identification. I could actually become the silent glistening snow under a white, icy moon or the storm-ravaged seas or calm waters shimmering with late-afternoon sun diamonds... my writing came pouring out, non-stop, and at a pace I could barely maintain. Words from everywhere visited upon me, and I welcomed their arrival as one would welcome a refuge in a storm. They became my mainstay, my fort against the disease and a safe harbor against the world. It was not the words alone, but the words intertwined with my imagination, and my determination to sustain my integrity, though it meant temporary avoidance of the disease hidden beneath the masks.

An unexpected side effect of my daily writing is the information that my neurologist gave to me during my most recent exam. He informed me that my Parkinson's has NOT progressed during the past year. It has maintained a stable course due, perhaps, to the increased activity of my brain from the writing, which may have possibly slowed down the expected loss of dopamine. Succinctly: increase the brain activity = slower loss of dopamine = maintenance of symptoms.

Fortunately, even at my age, I have not grown weary of writing and have learned to write simply, without tiresome explanations, and to speak lightly of sweet musings and whispers of tender love. With like compassion in mind, I hope my readers allow my lassitude of seven decades plus four to wear my masks to the ball and dance forevermore.

SYMPHONY OF SPRING

There can be no mistake. That's Spring Music all right. Nothing else sounds like it. It's not the low-pitched throaty strings of a cello, nor is it the blare of trumpets strutting in parade formation, and I don't think it's a tenor sax that usually slides in, between notes, unannounced. It's birds, of all kinds: Song Sparrows, Larks and Bobolinks who sing the introduction of our symphony, sounding like triangles, bells, small cymbals and chimes. They chirp in a high soprano pitch, somewhat slow tempo with an uncomplicated steady rhythm, often referred to as the "dawn chorus." Next, they are followed by a back-up chorus of altos consisting of Chickadees, Orioles and Wrens arriving in few numbers at first, then increasing steadily to a full sonorous counterpoint, similar to the woodwinds such as oboes and clarinets. An increased volume and faster pace catches your attention, and then an overlay of staccato from the flutes and piccolos (offered by woodpeckers and nuthatches of course), joined by two enthusiastic harps as performed by the nightingales, representing the sounds of trickling and gurgling waterfalls of melting ice and snow. The wind instruments are just that, the sounds of the new winds from the west mingling with little breezes from the east, followed by the major theme presented by the violins and violas, as sung by the owls, loons and whippoorwills, soaring, supporting and gliding into one climactic crescendo joined by an entire flock of robins.

Right now, I'm not sure if I'm in a Bambi movie singing "Zipadeedoodah," or I'm missing Jo Stafford belting out "It's spring again, and birds on the wing again, start to sing again, that old melody..."

But seriously, we all know that the sounds of spring are like music, and music can be as sweet as a new spring. (Before we stray too far, I recommend listening to a symphony entitled “The Pines of Rome” by Respighi. You really will hear those birds of which I spoke.)

Our symphony begins in early spring when the teasing new breeze from over the hill carries haunting melodies from great distances heard only in the back of your mind, when you’re half-awake and daydreaming in a favorite rocker on the back porch—an enjoyment which will probably be short-lived once Ethel finds you and reminds you of the vision she has of a new vegetable and flower bed, a vision blooming in her mind—and, of course, you can always find music to plant by, such as the dwarfs in “Snow White,” “Hi ho, hi ho; it’s off to work we go, tra la la la la...”

Spring is also in dire need of music to accompany the arrival of the flowers. Flowers! Flowers everywhere, and what better music to surround all the blooms than “The Waltz of the Flowers” from “The Nutcracker” ballet by Pyotr Ilyich Tchaikovsky? I mean, the flowers are even coming up from last year, and some from the year before, and I haven’t even planted one—this year!! Of course we all know that they are perennials, or bulbs your spouse buried into the ground last fall. Those that didn’t serve as supper or dessert for the rodents and cute little critters now start to poke around, as the crocuses begin to peek over the top of the garden bed to see if it’s safe to take their usual places before the hyacinths bully their fat bellies up into their allotted space only to be crowded out by chatterbox daffodils all dressed alike in yellow and white and sounding like backyard gossips straight from the song “Pick a Little/Talk a Little” sung by the ladies’ chorus in “Music Man.” And can’t you just see two rows of tall, majestic, scarlet tulips, 76 in all, representing the “76 Trombones”? Listen; I can almost hear them now.

Kids love spring, and some spring music belongs only to kids. What would we have done without kid’s songs like “Lavender’s Blue, Dilly Dilly, Lavender’s Green,” or “A-Tisket, A-Tasket, a Brown and Yellow Basket,” the Cinderella jump rope song, and how about “It’s Raining, It’s Pouring, the Old Man is Snoring,” etc... You take it from there...’cause there’s no end...

Music aside, for a moment, don’t you just love watching spring and little kids? Little kids, who on the first warm day almost bounce out of the house, find some dry pavement and then puddles!! Puddles there just for the splashing, especially since Mom said not to. But you can’t blame the kids. Spring made them do it. Spring makes little kids giggle and screech and chase each other and fall down and cry and then get up and start all over again.

Do you recall Gilbert and Sullivan? The music of those two genius fellows, those two grown-up kids, is equivalent to spring buttercups, not only the buttercups referred to in their lyrics, (‘I’m called little buttercup, dear little buttercup, though I could never tell why...) but in the light, frothy blooms, sprightly dance step, sweet pastel colors and wholly innocent operettas of romance and love and spring. (If you ask me though, a little bit of G & S has been known to carry over into summer and fall...and...)

Finally, spring will have a chance at its first hurrah, otherwise known as an early spring thunderstorm. Thunderstorms should be completely in the hands of some kettle drums or bigger, but for early storms, little drums would be fine. There is almost a certain daintiness about the new season that needs to gradually convince itself that it can, indeed, bellow and storm. Spring’s first thunder is somewhat comparable to a fragile little lady’s muffled sneeze covered by her lacey, light blue handkerchief—delicately waiting for a moment or two, carefully folding and properly replacing it. The entire event sounds like it should be a Chopin Prelude, carefully executed, full of melody, but not overwhelming. For contrast, do you remember when you were taking a walk on a sticky late afternoon with thick gray-black clouds, barely moving, hanging low overhead, maybe faintly rumbling, when suddenly the heavens erupted into a violent KA-BOOM, and the explosion of thunder shook the ground under your feet and left both knees wobbling. Now, *that's* a THUNDERSTORM!! And that would be Wagner!! Or, better yet, Shostakovich, one of those mighty Russian composers, who would really make all of us sit up and take notice! Try Shostakovich's Symphony No 10 if you doubt me. Of course, if you prefer, you can always connect with the Disney movie "Fantasia" presentation of "Night on Bald Mountain" by M. Mussorgsky, but a little too scary for our spring scenario.

Our Symphony of Spring comes to a close. The season quiets and draws itself into a slumber that awaits the dawn of summer. Spring is finished, will rest to the music of "Clair de Lune" by Claude Debussy and wait for the new season to begin.

LAST CHANCE TO GET INTO THAT BATHING SUIT BEFORE SUMMER ARRIVES DIET

You say there isn't a diet left that you haven't tried, and you absolutely refuse to try any more tofu, couscous or old goose sprinkled with bird seed, dried corn kernels or alfalfa stolen from the neighbor's cow pasture. Fine! I've got the "no-fail guaranteed-to-work diet plan" where all your adipose-in-repose tissue disappears or all your money refunded. Just follow the simple plan below, and you're on your way to the new old you (or was it the old new you?).

DAY ONE: The idea is to get your mind off of food. Don't battle it, don't fight it, just ignore it, avoid it and get your mind on something else, for instance, think about orange. Today is orange day. Eat only orange food, and drink only orange drinks, wear only orange-colored clothes, inside and out. You'll be so busy thinking orange that you'll forget about food (except maybe an orange). One little side effect is that you'll hate the color orange for the rest of your life; but there are lots of other colors.

DAY TWO: Self talk day. All day long, tell yourself, aloud, that you hate all food and will never eat again. Be firm. Convince yourself, and by the end of the day, you will have become anorexic (the fast-occurring form of the disease) and will be unable to eat a bite.

DAY THREE: Get up early so you can find a good shrink to treat your disorder, which now includes anxiety, dizziness and fainting spells due to lack of nourishment. You won't have time for eating because it will take all day trying to get a last-minute appointment.

DAY FOUR: Chew a lot day. Everything you put into your mouth must be chewed 865 times. You will quickly lose your appetite.

DAY FIVE: Stand on a busy street corner and shout insults and obscenities at all the passersby. Really shout at them, look fierce and angry. You will lose weight as you will not be able to eat until you get relief from the pain in your fractured nose, jaw and swollen eyes.

DAY SIX: Find a skinny person and follow that person closely for one day, observing what he/she eats. (You might want to take a few crackers with you so you'll have something to eat while you're in jail after your arrest for stalking.)

DAY SEVEN: Put on a bikini and stand in front of a full-length mirror for twenty minutes out of every hour and sing "Oh beautiful, for spacious thighs, for too much apple pie."

CONGRATULATIONS!! You have completed the diet!!

You might not have lost any weight, but we bet you met some nice people, er… with the exception of the ones who are suing you for defamation of character (relating to Day Five)… and what about that nice shrink with whom you finally got an appointment? Well, so he had a fake diploma—who's perfect?

If nothing else works, just try reciting this:
Diet, diet, who's got the diet?
That works every day, just tell me, and I'll buy
it.

I've supped on Atkins, Stillman and Optifast
From only eggs and carbs that left me with lots
of
—yearnings for potatoes and gravy and cake
That I promise I won't eat no matter what it
takes
Til I can get into that dress by Saturday night
Then I'll really start again and not take one
bite

But on second thought I need a new swim suit anyway.

SUMMER GOES TO SLEEP

Summer savors its final days, stretching out languidly, like a drowsy cat on the living room bay window, searching for the last rays of a sunny day, yawning and circling three times before choosing the warmest corner of the window and not the least bit embarrassed of its indolent mood brimming over with laziness.

Both summer and the cat are accustomed to settling into dreamy afternoons, desirous of attention but too self-satisfied to seek it out.

Both know how to rumble; summer in a low-pitched distant grumble of an approaching storm, while the cat will awaken when it pleases and will protest with a warning guttural purr-r-r should you even *think* about touching him before the natural cessation of his slumber.

At times, this past summer misbehaved like a spoiled child; day after day it smoldered and pouted, stubbornly becoming hotter and hotter, never giving in, as if daring the frantic parent to resort to stronger measures. It also coaxed the elderly to find secret cool places in hopes that their hideaways would go undetected by the fickle season, so eager, at times, to stomp its foot with storms of thunder followed by sweet rain and pastel rainbows arched in the sky.

Before hiding from long winter days, summer glances over its shoulder, wondering if the little kids with their painted metal pails and shovels have discovered the cooling lakes meant for splashing and filled their pails with sand; beat on it, turned it over, pounded the bottom and did it all over again and again and again. Summer wonders: "Did they do all that? Did they play long and hard enough?"

Summer continues to ponder: "Were there enough picnics? Were there picnics by the lake, the neighbor's backyard, the park by the playground and just about anyplace where you could grill a hot dog, red or white? Did Aunt Sue bring enough canned beans? Oh, enough," thinks summer, "I'll have to leave that up to Aunt Sue."

The hottest season of them all, summer may coyly withhold cool breezes for the sake of promoting closeness and friendliness. For instance, without invitation, it will settle in upon the neighborhood after the kids are "put down" for the night. With no air conditioning, the kids in the upstairs rooms of a two-story house kick off the blankets and try to cool off while falling asleep to the incessant cicadas' or locusts' gossip and goings-on of night-time shenanigans. The relentless heat motivates the ladies to locate their colorful paper fans won at a state fair, share them with others and sit on the front stoop and sweep the air briskly across their hot, moist faces, all the while increasing their chatter and story telling. The heat lightning flickers in the distance reflecting upon their shiny glistening cheeks. Most passersby are sure to say: "It's the humidity, you know, the humidity and not the heat..."

Did summer nights provide that tempting background of sighs of passion and love as found in a small art movie theater showing one of those black-and-white foreign films with lots of trickling beads of sweat, and even if it was in French, you knew they were saying, "Ah, adore me, my cherie, I'm yours."

Blossoming love is almost synonymous with summer for it seems to understand that romance clings to the scent of honeysuckle drifting into a lonely room on a late night breeze, teasing one's imagination and causing the flimsy moon-drenched curtains at the window to flutter and whisper words heard only in private declarations of love.

The honeysuckle perfume may linger, teasing and coaxing the mind to believe in make-believe, when suddenly and all too soon, like a false admirer, it responds to a new entreaty to the stars above overheard from the meadows below, then with promises of enticing rendezvous, the intoxicating aroma leaves the senses spinning as it joins the music of the night and replaces young love's tears with the stark light of daybreak.

Summer loves to compare itself with other seasons. With a haughty, disdainful, even arrogant shrug, it discredits the pale yellow of spring's attempt to color the landscape as insipid, timid and without inspiration.

"Why," summer boasts, "why can't it just step forward and BLOOM, instead of offering such an apologetic display?" For comparison, summer boasts: "Just look at my troops of tall sunflowers lined up solidly with petals of gold surrounding a sun-bronzed face, guarding the fields from undesirable visitors. Where else would you see such a display, such majesty?"

There is no end to the artistry and talents of summer. Look for the golden fields of marigolds—marigolds of deep yellow, marigolds of bright orange, each flower full of thick petals pressed gently together, which, when grown en mass, create a blanket of glittering jewels beneath a tranquil sky. It is hard to turn away, but summer beckons us on.

Summer invites you to rest awhile on a bench in a secluded garden meant for quiet and repose, one that has been filled with white and yellow daisies, pink poppies and lavender sweet peas, all nearby, while at your feet little pansy faces smile. They smile in repose, they smile in the quiet, and they smile again while you take in a deep breath allowing the fusion of images and scents to enter your being. If, at this point, you close your eyes and still see the pansies smiling, you have acquired a beginning step in relaxation. Good for you. Stay for a while, breathe deeply, and enjoy the flowers with your eyes closed.

Our last garden stop is to view an artist's study in delicacy, a weaver's fashion of intricate laces, and the hypnotist's picture of imagination, otherwise known as a flower named Queen Anne's Lace. To view it from afar, across a wide field, is to behold a sea of stars scattered across a late evening sky. Summer means fields and fields of Queen Anne's Lace, row upon row with all different heights. To view them up close is to see layers of white flowers comprised of tiny white flowers swaying gracefully in a gentle wind. The spectacular relative of a carrot is summer's tour de force to the waning season.

Having sat by summer's side and observed its manners, rituals, presents and punishments, I have not yet understood its mysteries, its beauty, nor its sorrows. Perhaps we're not meant to. Perhaps if I were to ask summer how it sees us, we might gain a clearer vision of its perspective.

In response to my inquires, I will need to expand upon my imagination and suppose that summer has this to say, "I've shown and displayed my majestic empire and offered dreams and fantasies that were yours for the taking. For you I have whispered songs of poetry to nurture young love as well as the love of many years to come. For you, I have spread the scents of the orient and moons that have seen Arabian nights before you.

"I am not just an accumulation of a few months clumped together, I am a world unto myself. I am spread out before you in all my regal sights and sounds, just waiting for you to notice and become intimate with my pulse, my rhythms, my role in the universe, my eternal existence.

"Now, is the time for me to rest and allow the autumn leaves their cloaks of splendor and the snows of tomorrow a sure path to your door."

Summer goes to sleep.

ARE YOU AUTUMN OR FALL?

Autumn is the distant storm on the horizon waiting
impatiently
To unleash its fury once the leaves have taken flight.
Autumn is for poets who see the colors melding into
sensuous
Crimsons and velvety burnt orange, swirling with brilliant
Reds, quieted by pale yellows and reconciled by gold.
Autumn is for a pot-bellied moon hanging low in the early
sky,
Full and bursting over with harvest-time promises.
Autumn is for one last kiss on a bed of musky leaves
Still warmed by memories of summer's farewell breeze.

Autumn is also a time of loss. It's a time to let go, to not hold
fast
But to unfurl and relinquish all that has gone before.
Autumn is a time to measure the tears that have lingered in
sorrow,
Too long for use, too sad for recall.
Autumn will be easier half-way through, when the fog lifts
and
Bittersweet images bring comfort once more, when
New dreams, though unknown, yet tender, will begin again.

Fall is brats and beer and brawn and belches,
It's shoulder pads and pigskin and tightened haunches.
It's cheerleaders and mascots drawing the line,
It's chili and tailgate fixin's and chants and cheers.
Fall is the chill in the air and old sweaters and caps
And folks thinking about packing up and heading out

Anywhere—where bathing suits and sunshine combine.
So, are you Fall —the mighty gas-powered leaf blower?
Or are you Autumn? —a whimsical Quixote swinging your
rake
At the stars while you swing at the leaves?

WHEN THE POLLYWOGS PLAYED AND THE DANDELIONS FLEW

It was late in the spring when the dandelions
Exchanged their golden cloaks for
White gossamer wings and lazily flew
Far above the sunlit meadow.
Did you watch them drift by?

April rain filled the ponds where the pollywogs played.
"Do they really become toads?" asked we.
"Tis so," chirped the crickets, "and if you give them a kiss,
Then one day, princes they'll be."

Where's the hopscotch chalk
And my old skate key?
Remember how I flew down that hill?
We used to jump rope with Cinderella and her fella
Maybe they have my roller-skate key.

Violets demur, pansies shy faces,
Sweet Peas smiling coquettishly.
Lilies of the Valley chattering in the shade
"Watch out! Here come the tulips,
They'll take over everything."

Spring whispers in my ear,
"Olly Olly Oxen Free"
If you look for me you'll find me
Where wishes were reality and yesterday was new,
When the pollywogs played and the dandelions flew.

WHY NOT?

Why not go with me to the
Far regions of my mind where on
Wings of Aurora, etched in gold and
Stretched in flight, we'll soar
Wildly into hurricanes of blue.
Why Not?

Why not hold one another throughout the night
And dream of comets colliding and exploding
Into starbursts of meteors and moons
Spinning crazily over celestial plains
Before reality finds us and captures us—
Why Not?

Why not gather all our tears
And put them away in that dwelling
Where we stored all our pain
When we could no longer endure
And would wait for our resolve to regain—
Why Not?

Why not fathom all your being to
Search for me if I am lost and
Deserted by all who once loved me,
Why not enclose me in a space within you
That would hold us both for eternity
Why Not?

THE POND IN SPRING

Follow me through fields of red poppies and buttercups,
Gather yellow dandelions under a warm yellow sun.
Cold sparkling rain will cascade down your face
For sweet spring has arrived on dragonfly wings.

The crickets are hiding in wild strawberry patches,
Pollywogs are swimming in the pond.
The soft yielding earth gives way to slender grasses
Bending and waving to meadowlarks on the wing.

A sleepy rabbit nods by the edge of the pond,
Blinking into still waters that shimmer and glitter
With sun diamonds singing in the late afternoon:
"Close your eyes, your little eyes, close your eyes."

It was spring when I sang to my new baby cooing
And we would pass by cattails dressed in brown velvet coats,
Standing like sentinels along the path to the pond
Showing us the way as we strolled along.

Come with me when dusk is in the meadow and
Clusters of evening stars are dancing in the pond,
When the owl summons the little ones to their nests
And the whippoorwill chases the moon and greets the sun.

DREAMS

I dreamt of a celestial vessel of emerald crystals and ruby stones
That swept me into its hold filled with sapphires and gold
And sailed beyond the moon, behind the sun
And over the stars. I transcended the sea of northern lights,
The rhapsodies of muses and dances of the spheres
Then drifted through the Milky Way until we
Reached the sea of morning and evening stars.

I dreamt I felt the warmth of the sun as I lay on a reef by a quiet lagoon
Where trade winds caressed my senses with exotic perfumes.
White and black swans glided by the shore and hummed soothing
Lullabies until nightfall blackened the sky.
Then came Artemis, Goddess of Light, who poured down stars between the tall
Reaching pines that embraced the lights in their arms of
Soft branches, swaying quietly, whispering throughout the night.

I dreamt of a storm-ravaged sea
Of waves cascading towards the sand, collapsing,
Dispersing, withdrawing again and again,
Of wild pounding explosions resounding from the deep
Then suddenly exhausted, crashing across the sand
Only to rise again, regaining their strength
And cresting into tumultuous throes, unwilling to let go.

Dreams are fantasy; illusions seek reality
And wishes are forgotten before the moon is new.
The curtains of the most majestic stage of all slowly
Draw back to reveal a glowing orange ball
Gradually encroaching upon a pale grey
Sky while new worlds, on the threshold of tomorrow
Lie waiting in the wings.

LITTLE KIDS' SNOW

Kids' snow is different than grown-up snow.
Grown-up snow knows where it's going,
And neatly piles up into mounds and icy hills.
Kids' snow is fluffy and swirly and falls and
Tumbles everywhere, never sure of where it's going.

Kids' snow gets on your boots and
Turns to mud so you get hollered at
When it dries and falls off
When you bring it into the house.
Grown-up snow drips dry on a rubber mat.

Kids' snow sparkles and twinkles and glitters
Then melts on your tongue when it first comes down.
You can make angels in Kids' snow,
But not so in grown-up snow 'cause they can't get up.

Only Kids' snow sticks to your mittens
And cakes into hard clumps when it gets wet.
Grown-up snow is not allowed to stay on gloves
And is brushed off a coat before it melts
When they're brushing, they always say "tsk, tsk, tsk."

I love little Kids' snow. One day it's an igloo
And the next a frozen pond or a smiling
Fat snowman with a broom on his arm.
One day I asked the snowman:

"When I'm all grown up, will there still be little Kids' snow?"
He just kept on smiling and never did answer me,

But I'll bet he knows,
He just looks like he knows.

LITTLE KIDS' SUMMER

Summer is all mine.
I'm not going to share it with anyone
I'll get out my biggest yellow ball
With the blue stripes and bounce it
So hard I'll never hear my mother call me
For dinner I don't want any anyways.

In summer I don't have to go to school
So I act like a snot that's what
My sister calls me but I don't care
'Cause she's one too I'll find a ripe
Dandelion and blow it in her face
And maybe it'll go up her nose – hah!

Sometimes my parents torture me (my sister too)
We have to put on our swim suits
Run across the hot sand on our bare feet
To get to the ocean it burns just awful
We scream and yell but they never listen
'Cause they would just as soon sell us anyways.

On some summer nights there are dancing colored
Lights flashing across the sky.
My father says they're the northern lights
They take my breath away but I think
They should come with music.
My father says they do; just listen.

I'll give you back one part of the summer
I don't like thunder and lightning.

Little Kid's Summer

I heard grown ups say there's thunder
Because air rushes in to fill a vacuum
Now, I've heard of everything!
My mom's gotta vacuum the sky?!

Summer's going fast but I don't care
'Cause I'm not going back to school
I decided to stay home and grow up in my bedroom
When I told my parents they just smiled
Kinda funny and looked at the ceiling
They do that a lot lately; the older I get the more
They look at the ceiling. I wonder why.

THE PROMISE OF AUTUMN

Oh, you lush September and sweet October
With your shy ways, yet dressed in the flaming colors
Of a wanton lady.
How you have teased me all of my life, from your
Earthy damp scent of leaves raked into piles of joy
Just waiting for the playful child who spies it first.
You provoked, you coaxed and beckoned me to come
Close to pick up your leaves and fall in love with them,
So much so, I had to glue them into a book
To gaze and gaze at the colors until they faded
And crackled into little bits.

The height of the season welcomes the arrival of the
Breathless sight of a gold maple in full dress,
Sticking out its chest and bragging of its majesty for all to see.
You can almost hear it saying: "See me, admire me—
I'm the most beautiful of all."
However, that may not be so, for if there's a dark red Oak by its side, the two can really become quite conceited.

I will peak with you this year. I will watch you as
You blush into full regalia, then like you,
I will rest awhile, let the colors ebb as each leaf, almost
Unwillingly, lets go and quietly meanders, an uncharted path
Towards the waiting arms of an earth that too soon
Turns away from its warmth and gives
The cold shoulder of early winter.
On second thought, maybe I'll wait for your

Performance next Autumn. Who knows what you will
Have in store for us then?

ALFRED DOESN'T COME BY THIS WAY ANYMORE

Winter winds howl through the frigid night
Bending the crackling tree branches and pursuing
The owl in its flight, as it swoops across the white face
Of the moon and over the silver snow.
The bony clasp of wrenching cold
Sinks into old folks' limbs still
Aching from winter's descent often spoken of in hushed and
Whispered tones: "Remember that winter of '72?"

Spring needs to jostle the earth and herald the sun
For the snow is leaving, and the robins are returning
To take their bows for their timely announcement
Of all things warm and soft and fragrant and young.
Old folks throw off their shawls and discard their frowns
And try on that flimsy blouse and lavender lace gown
Then dance to a tune heard only in their heads
A few springtimes ago, that visits now and again,
Through darkened pathways and corridors of the mind
Until the melody becomes an echo of the youth that was left
behind.

Ever seen a thunderstorm lashing and whipping
About in wild fury with lightning streaking
Like a venomous tongue 'cross a darkened sky?
No? Then meet my neighbor, another old folk,
Who imitates the thunderbolt when her ire is provoked
Pity the morning newsboy who's late with the edition
Or any poor fellow lest he practice contrition
When dealing with the neighborhood grouch

Albeit, she can charm when she has to,
But it's been a long time, and besides why bother?
Alfred doesn't come by this way anymore.
Maybe next summer.

Autumn is the messenger of change and a sense of expectation
Permeates the chilled mist of early dawn.
The broad strokes and splashes of emerging colors
Predict the return engagement about to begin
Inspiring a command performance by the artist and his palette,
A cornucopia of images for the poet and his pen
Or a reminder for older folks that changes
Are not ours to declare or orchestrate as we choose,
Nor do we audition or select the players of our lives,
Or is the staging assembled for our approval.
Our challenge is to accept and play out our role,
Though at times, it may seem like an insurmountable goal.

Old folks are an enigma and difficult to fathom, except
I know that as the seasons pass us by, so our lives in cycles spin,
And like a Merry-go-round we're caught in the thrill of the ride,
Unsure how we boarded and when it will end,
We shout to the conductor, as we reach for the golden ring:
"Let's go around again!!!"

WINTER WALTZ

The leaves through my window
Are dressed in green
With a splash of show-off red
In the corner, just waiting to be seen,
Rustling with impatience to fly away from
Winter quietly crouched around the bend.

Morning bolts of sun charge through the branches,
Noisy and bright and stark
Surprising the sleepy little ones
In their beds of down and warmth.

The winds coax and tease the
Tremulous leaves as they sail by
In pursuit of my left-over dreams,
Dreams too old for recall, yet
Too new for hiding under lock and key.

Like a restless inept suitor,
Winter blusters an unannounced and
Clumsy arrival, thrashes about with fury,
Then exhausted and spent, finally
Releases its grip and like a gentleman
At the ball, bids for a waltz with the enchanted
Lady of Spring, who waits demurely
And knowingly in the wings. She smiles, dances
For a moment or two, then gracefully
Shows him the door.

A FORGOTTEN VALENTINE

Every writer has an excuse for not meeting a deadline,
Hence, I spare you mine. Suffice it to say that while
browsing
My poems I found the following old Valentine.
It's a trifle overdue, but the sentiment is still true,
For although the writer's a year older—
the recipient is too.

We've smooched and hugged and tickled and grinned,
Rolled our eyes and fussed 'til the cows came in.
We screamed and shouted and purred and pouted,
Been ecstatic, romantic, arthritic and dumbfounded.
We've held hands even while alone at night,
Been overwhelmed, understated, misquoted and
underrated.
We've admired and respected our mutual pluses
And mostly can't remember why all the silly fusses.
We've minimized, discredited and patted a cheek or two,
We've supported, upheld and bit our tongue 'til we're blue.
We've tsked, sighed, grumbled and scowled,
Been cutesy and sweet, flirty and foul.
So here's the end of our little review,
We did okay, not perfect, but we'll do.
It all adds up, and it's simple to say—
You're my Valentine, (and I'm yours) forever and always.

’TIS SPRING—TRA LA

I’ll slip into spring, if it pleases me,
I’ll wear white before its time
With open-toe shoes tripping o’er the snow
And sing way up high if it pleases me.
Tra La

‘Tis Spring again, so I’ll flirt
With all the fellows who have spring
In their step and romance in their soul
And should one ask me to wed, I’ll run
Through the daffodils ’til he catches me,
If it pleases me, or I’ll just let him run on ahead.
Tra La

I’ll swing lazily in the hammock and watch
Translucent wings of dragonflies shimmer
Through streams of golden light and promise myself
That tomorrow I’ll plant my dreams ’midst
The roses and violets and then wait and see
Which ones will bloom and which will fade:
The roses, my dreams, the violets, or me?
Tra La

DO YOU HAVE A RETURN POLICY?

The first time I heard what sounded like the rattling of metal chain links echoing in an ancient dungeon, it was mostly a faint sound, growing louder, then soft again. I had left work early to do some more Christmas shopping, arrived home to a quiet, empty house, plopped on the sofa, thrown off my shoes with a deep sigh, and it started again. "Clang Clang rattle pause; Clang Clang rattle pause."

"Sounds like it's coming from upstairs," I informed myself, "maybe a mouse—no, a squirrel—no, a woodchuck in the wall—maybe." I was about to investigate when it stopped, and I reminded myself to tell John, when he comes home, about the mystery unfolding above me. Of all nights for him to be working late. In addition to that, I'm dead-tired and shouldn't let my imagination take flight. A woodchuck! Really! Why not a 200-pound mouse! I smiled at my silliness. I must really be tired!

The next sound I heard was of someone getting punched in the belly—like "UGH - UGH - UGH" followed by the sound of a long intake of air and scuffling sounds and "OH – OH – O – O – OH – OH."

That does it! Now I'm scared! Someone or some people had broken into our house and were trying to remove the furniture, although I couldn't quite figure out why, considering the market value of Grandma's old bed, but whoever was up there sounded like he/they needed a helper. All right, this is a no-brainer, dummy, just call 911 NOW!

WHAM POUND POUND — WHAM POUND — SOUND OF FEET DRAGGING — OH! I'VE HAD IT!! FEET DRAGGING HEAVILY DOWN THE STAIRS! THEY'RE COMING DOWN THE STAIRS AFTER ME!

I ran into the kitchen, looked around quickly for a weapon, didn't see any knives, and the only thing I saw was a plunger in the sink. I grabbed it and hid behind the kitchen door, plunger poised in the air, ready to strike! I waited.

Silence. Sounds of heavy breathing followed by more "OH – OH – OH." Maybe the creature, or whatever, was worn out from exertion while trying to steal our stuff. Oh, if only that was true. My heart started pounding as the "CREAK, WHINE, SCRAPE ON METAL" resumed, and I decided to get down on the floor and shimmy to the phone in the living room. I got to the phone and with my shaking hands, tried to dial the numbers, while visualizing metal chains being wound around my heaving chest. Finally, I heard a voice say "This is 911." I opened my mouth to respond, and I simply croaked, unable to speak. "OH – WHERE'S JOHN?" I didn't realize I had screamed his name until I looked up at him standing at the top of the staircase and then running down the stairs to help me, asking: "Honey, what on earth is the matter?"

"NO!! DON'T GO UP THERE!! There is a monster or groups of robbers or a sex-crazed fiend just waiting to whack us or murder us in our work clothes. You've got to get something to hit them with, but wait a minute—what are you doing? Why are you in gym clothes, and you're all sweaty, what's going on here? You're supposed to be working late, and what are you doing upstairs?"

"Whoa—slow down," John advises. "First of all, we're not about to get whacked, as you say. There was no one upstairs except me, assembling your exercise and deluxe gym set Christmas gift and trying it out…"

"My what?"

"Your surprise Christmas present."

"But, but, you said 'an exercise machine' for me?"

"Right, honey, I knew you'd be thrilled!"

"But wait, your car was not in the garage, so I thought you were working late. How did you ever get this piece of machinery in here?"

"I couldn't get it all into our car," John explained, "so Marty used his truck and helped me set it up. Gee, honey, I meant to surprise you on Christmas morning, not scare you tonight. I thought we could start out exercising together first thing in the morning and get a head start on our New Year's resolutions."

"Uh... oh sure; that's a real good idea, and there's nothing I'd rather have..."

"Good, honey," John urges, "c'mon, let's go upstairs so you can see what I'm talking about."

There in the middle of our spare room was a giant apparatus with a huge bright red ribbon around it and all kinds of attachments, chairs, bells and whistles and doohickeys that would certainly account for most of the noises.

"But what about the heavy breathing and the moaning sounds that I heard?"

"Well, sweetheart," replied John, "it has been a while since I've worked out. But wait a minute, while we're asking questions, wasn't that a plunger I saw on the floor at the bottom of our stairs?" What were you planning to do with that? Death by plunger?"

"Oh, uh...uh...uh... well, it was the only thing I saw, and anyway, never mind that. Don't you think we had better rest up before we start using my present on Christmas morning? I really can't wait to start exercising. Really! I'm just thrilled...wouldn't want anything else. Uh, where did you say you bought it?

I'LL BE RIGHT THERE

My husband and I, for the past several years, have enjoyed a compatible relationship, sharing similar interests, activities and friends. Lately, however, we seem to have entered into some weird behaviors which I find quite irritating and annoying. I think I'm usually a calm and even-tempered individual, but I am not able to accept his mistress, a multi-talented, brilliant, seductive tease, capable of delivering all sorts of temptations and surprises. Worst of all, this creature has snared and captured the victim; he has become helpless and addicted.

There may be other names for this Lorelei, but I call it a variety of names, none of which are very complimentary. My husband, Harvey, lovingly refers to it as his "computer darling." He is very proud that he built it himself and even referred to it, jokingly, I presume, as his "baby." Whenever I've retired for the night and am lying in our bed, alone, waiting for him to join me, I'll call out, "Harvey! Aren't you coming to bed?"

Throughout the darkened hallways, a voice echoes from afar, "I'll be right there," and I will admit my level of patience is decreasing as my cache of irritability increases. The phrase "I'll be right there" has become entirely too familiar and, sadly, what often follows his reply is his absence. Of course, his relationship with his computer is not just during the evening, but thrives throughout the weekends and days off from work, as well.

This all started about six months ago. (What must the neighbors think about our nocturnal exchanges at a rather loud volume throughout the late night and early morning hours?) Can you, or any sane person, see yourself in a darkened, quiet, still house with only a faint bluish light dancing behind closed windows and under closed doors while you become almost motionless, neither eating nor drinking, while your face slowly becomes pale, sallow and drawn? After a while, your vital signs slow down, your breathing becomes labored and raspy, and you gradually descend into an ever-weakening state, and the only sound escaping from the computer room is a muffled "I'll be right there..."

Of course, I'm exaggerating a bit about his physical condition. He's not quite that bad—but not far from it. I know Harvey loves me more than his computer, but just listen to what I'm thinking! Am I really comparing myself with a machine?

On a recent early morning, near dawn, while lightly sleeping, which is all I ever do lately, I heard Harvey scuffle his poorly-nourished, skinny, slippered feet into our bedroom. At least, I think it was him, as I caught only a brief glimpse, which is all I ever get lately. He looked so weary and awful that I decided I need to do something—but what?

One of us has to change our behavior, and it doesn't look like it's going to be Harvey. It appears that all my shouting and reaction to his condition is not going to have very much effect, so I'll have to change my approach. I'll stop calling him to come to bed. Eventually, he'll become exhausted and find his way. I'll just wait and see what happens.

For a long time, nothing happened, and I didn't know where he slept, on the floor, in a chair, or who knows where. Then finally, my waiting was rewarded, and I could hear him now, a shuffling sound, scuffing slowly down the hall.

"Harvey, is that you?" I asked.

"Humpf, fah, uh, whausfumuf," he said, as if in a stupor.

"Harvey, why don't you get into bed and get some sleep, and then let's talk in the morning?"

For a moment, he looked at me with anger, and his eyes seemed to have a very strange appearance. I'm sure it must have been my tired state, but for an instant I could swear his pupils looked like two computer icons—those little symbols that appear on a screen when you first turn it on. I did a double take, then felt as though I was about to scream or panic, for as fast as the images appeared, they vanished. I could only hear my sudden intake of air, and then I heard him say, as though with great effort: "Right, food, eat morning, better…," and then he collapsed upon the bed.

I studied his features as he began to fall asleep, concentrating on what appeared to be new growth of hair around his mouth, over his upper lip, not heavy, but rather like slender wisps of hair. I reminded myself to check it out in the morning when I could see better without waking him. I had no idea he was growing a mustache.

In brighter light, Harvey looked awful. His mustache looked more like slender short whiskers, and his overall color was pale grey. How could I have not noticed before now? I think I was nourishing my anger instead of nourishing Harvey. I felt a pang of guilt, blaming myself for his condition, and right then, I started a campaign to cure Harvey of whatever habit, addiction or ailment he had acquired.

For the ensuing weeks, I relentlessly enforced a new schedule of healthier habits and lifestyle. He agreed to limit his time at the computer, began to take short exercise breaks and eat only the nutritious meals I prepared for him. I noticed how he seemed to lean towards high protein foods such as cheese—be it cheese omelet, grilled cheese sandwiches or cheese and crackers and peanut butter, a lot of peanut butter. But I knew it was a high protein food, so I encouraged it.

Through all of this unwelcomed adventure, Harvey had still been able to keep his job, although I have no idea how his performance was evaluated, or how many of his job hours were devoted to his obsession. Of course, it was obvious to me that he had probably used most of his time off for illness or for vacation hours allotted to him for the numerous days he stayed at home at the computer. One thing, for sure, I know that I had never been on any vacation with him. He still spent several hours a day at that machine, but he never told me exactly what it was that lured him so and with such fascination. Sometimes I would hear weird noises or grunts from the computer room, and once, when I unexpectedly opened the door, I swear I saw, in the dim half-darkened room, those icons again, where his pupils once were. He quickly covered his face with both of his hands, and to my shock and horror, each one of his hands looked like a furry computer mouse (or whatever you call that thing). A scream stuck in my throat, because as soon as the images appeared, they disappeared, and Harvey calmly inquired, "What in the world are you staring at?"

I stammered, "Your hands. Look at your hands."

He held them out in front of him, and they appeared to be absolutely normal.

I quickly walked, and then half ran, away from him and the computer room, doubting what I thought I saw, especially in view of his placid and unruffled demeanor. For too many instances now, I have excused his appearance by telling myself I am overtired and in need of rest. Finally, such rationalizations would no longer satisfy me. I resolved to unravel the strange and unexplainable behaviors in this household.

I could not understand why he rarely changed his clothes in front of me anymore. Whenever he disrobed or got dressed, he used a small dressing room near his closet.

I attributed his behavior to an explanation of convenience, but would he always change in that one room and never change in any other place? How would this behavior relate to a possible addiction or strong ties to a computer? After his shower, where once he would walk casually around the bedroom, he now dried himself and dressed only in his changing room.

Harvey has also changed his choice of clothes while at home. He wears several layers of sweat shirts with hoods and sweat pants, covering himself almost completely, explaining he is cold. However, if I suggest turning up the thermostat, he will disagree.

I took my research a bit further and one evening, when he had fallen asleep, I cautiously touched his chest and back, which until now, had become an almost impossible gesture because of his style of clothing. Where Harvey was once almost entirely bare, it seemed as though I was touching some soft downy, maybe even fuzzy hair. He made a muffled sound of annoyance and quickly turned over. I would have to postpone my exploration until some other time.

During the weeks that followed, I kept a closer watch than usual, until finally, one night, everything came to a turning point. He left the door to the computer room slightly ajar, and in the half-dim light, as my eyes slowly became accustomed to it, he looked straight at me, and I, without a doubt, saw those computer icons instead of his eyes and his mouse-shaped furry black hands. I bolted from the door, and as I ran to the kitchen, I shouted, "Harvey, I need to talk to you—NOW!

Harvey slowly appeared: "Did you want something?" he asked, as calmly as though I had just asked if he wanted a cup of coffee.

"Harvey, you know as well as I do that there's something weird going on with your eyes and hands, or there was just a minute ago. Now you look normal, but you sure didn't a few moments ago. What is happening? Oh, I'm so upset I don't know what to think. I'm so confused, Harvey —talk to me! "

"Susan, I'm so sorry. I know I've been acting weird, but I just couldn't tell you that for the past couple months I have slowly become obsessed with the computer games, even addicted to talking on-line to others, but especially the games. I couldn't wait to get home each day so I could get to the computer. There were a number of times I wanted to tell you, but you know I'm not much for talking, so it became easier for me to develop an attachment to the computer."

"Harvey, I don't believe it! How could I not have known; not have realized it? I guess I was so wrapped up and feeling lonely, neglected and sorry for myself, I just didn't see it. But what about some of the weird things I saw, like your pupils looking like computer icons…and…?"

"That's easy to explain and kind of stupid," Harvey replied. "When I joined CAA a few months ago..."

"Wait a minute," I interrupted, "what's CAA?"

"Oh," explained Harvey, "it's Computer Addicts Anonymous, which is an organization like Alcoholics Anonymous. They help others like me with their addictions to computers. We attend as many meetings as we want and talk about our addiction problems. I swear I never saw this coming, and I've had a real tough time kicking it. I didn't want to tell you about it until I had a better handle on it."

Wiping away my tears, but still upset, I asked: "But what about your eyes?"

Harvey replied, somewhat sheepishly, "They were just silly glasses someone passed around at one of the meetings, as a joke, and I guess in a dark room, they look worse than they really are. I remember one night I forgot I had them on, and I must have really startled you when I finally went to bed. The black computer mouse gloves were distributed for those whose hands get cold after many hours at the computer. We all bought some T-shirts with fuzzy hair just to emphasize our non-mousy, strong determination."

I started to smile, and then with a little laugh, said: "For a while I was actually starting to think that maybe you were being transformed into...into...oh, I don't know what I'm saying."

"Susan, I'm so sorry. I never meant to scare you. In fact, you are the person who is mostly responsible for my recovery. It all started when you said you were going to take care of me and put me on a schedule of normal living routines, and I definitely needed something forceful in order to start a new life. I'll always love you and be grateful for your caring."

"Oh, Harvey, I love you too. I feel so much better. And while we're trying to straighten all this out, let's agree to spend more time with each other and at least go to bed together most nights. I've really started to miss you when you don't retire until I'm sound asleep."

"That sounds great, Susan. I'll be there, and that's a promise! This time I don't mean it the way I used to when I said, 'I'll be right there...'"

I added: "And you'll stop wearing all those long sweat pants and sweat shirts with those attached hoods that cause me never to see you anymore?" Before Harvey could answer, I continued: "Maybe if you start an exercise program, you'll be more active and you'll warm up and not get so cold that you need those extra warm clothes."

"Susan," Harvey replied, "you have some good ideas. I'm really lucky to have someone like you caring for me."

"Well, I'm sure we're going to beat this. Do you think that maybe we should both attend the CAA meetings?"

"The what? Oh, the CAA meetings. You bet. We'll go to the very next one, and that's a date! I promise!"

I waited for several weeks before deciding to remind Harvey about his promise. Then one chilly evening I suggested that we take our new books and go to bed early for some relaxing reading, and then I would ask about the meetings.

I showered first and was brushing my hair at my dressing table when Harvey stepped out of his dressing room wearing a new, large, hooded robe with a black satin twisted cord at the waist. As he walked by me, I noticed the cord had fallen and was trailing from underneath his robe. I thought that was rather strange, so I said:

"Here, wait a minute, Harvey, I'll get it." And, as I lifted my foot to step on the cord, Harvey shouted: "No, Susan, don't step on that!"

"Why not," I said and pounced on the cord. Harvey shouted "AGH – AUGH – SQUEEL-L-L – SQUEEK!!! SQUEE-E-E-E-K!!!! SQUE-E-E-E-L!!!!

"HARVEY!! YOU'RE NOT – CONNECTED – TO IT …ARE YOU?

"Harvey," I whispered, "is – that – you?"

JENNY'S TURN

Grandma Jenny has a natural kind of prettiness, no beauty queen winner, but pretty to look at just the same. She has taken good care of herself, is trim, and no one would suspect that she's a grandmother of twins. She just looks too young. Jenny was generally soft-spoken except when calling the family in for dinner, and then her strong voice would carry over the corn field.

Jenny had lived in the country all her life, where people would refer to their "kin folk" and a heavy rain storm as a "gully washer." Grandma Jenny was focused upon her family and neighbors. She bore a definite aura of pride in her child's shiny clean hair and starched pinafores. She would never admit to being "just a housewife," and when it was time to "put up" peaches, hers always took first or second place at the County Fair. Her family was never far away, and though the children are grown now, her grandchildren are still little, and they enjoy their almost daily visits with Grandma Jenny.

However, change is inevitable, and she and her husband, Tom, have been experiencing periods of unrest. Tom, who recently retired, is handling this early stage of adjustment described as: follow the wife around and ask her what she is doing every five minutes!

Jenny, however, has been preoccupied thinking about how she will spend her remaining years. She has reflected on her long hours of farm work and family work and feels, at a gut level, she needs to do something that is for her and her only. She realizes that her thoughts must sound awfully selfish, but she has a feeling of "now or never!"

She has formulated a plan and is hopeful that today, before the arrival of the family, she'll be able to approach Tom with the general idea she has been nourishing. She anticipates meeting with him as she stands by the back screen door, breathing in the moist fall air and hugging her folded arms tightly as if to ward off any negative vibes. She muses over her plan and even has a hard time believing it herself—go back to school!? A grandmother in a classroom with 18-year-olds? My heavens, I'm menopausal, and they're just babies. And what about Sally Jean and the twins? Who will baby-sit the little ones when Sally and Bill go to work? I just know they'll be upset with me. What if after a while, she continued to worry, they won't see me very often and then not even recognize me?

"Looks like an awfully interesting daydream, Jenny."

"Oh, Tom, you surprised me. I was hoping we could talk for a few minutes before the kids arrive for dinner."

"Sure, what's my girl got on her mind?"

"Well, do you remember I told you about an article that addressed the subject of fulfillment? It said that if you have a yearning to begin a career or fulfill a dream, you'll be a happier person if you try, even if you don't succeed. But if you don't even make an attempt to pursue your goal, then you may be left with a feeling of emptiness and confusion—as if planning a trip with no destination or directions."

Tom had been listening carefully and replied, "This isn't the first time we've talked about this, but you sound more serious this time. You're reminding me of a picture I saw of a little girl standing in front of a toy store window at Christmas time with a sad look on her face. I don't want you to feel like that; always on the outside looking in. Do you think you're ready to start some classes in creative writing? You have done some good work, you know."

"Oh, Tom, you sound supportive, and I do need your support, but what about the twins and baby-sitting? I just know that Sally and Bill will be upset with us...and what about your dinner?"

"My dinner? You mean if you go back to school, I will be denied an evening meal?" Tom teased.

"No, of course not, but some evenings I may be much later than I am now, or on really late nights, I'll have to leave something in the oven for you."

"C'mon Jen, let's not worry about stuff like that. We'll take care of the problems as they arise, as we always have. And about the twins, well, our kids may not prefer the new situation, but they're pretty level-headed, and I think they'll accept it and even adjust. Don't forget, they're our kids."

Jenny felt a surge of excitement as she heard a car approach the driveway. She has always valued their loving relationships, and she hopes that her announcement today will not seriously affect their feelings. There is a low rumbling of evening thunder prompting a sense of foreboding, and Jenny is unsure whether to shrug it off or take it seriously. She wonders to herself: "Am I doing the right thing?" The thunder continues, as if responding to her unanswered question.

Sally Jean and Bill stepped out of the car and shouted their "hellos" as the twins ran up the walk to Grandma's opened waiting arms. Jenny could feel her heart open to the little ones and prayed that that feeling would never change. "Come on in and sit down," Jenny said as she motioned to the dining table that Tom had set for the Autumn season with her favorite tablecloth and colorful fiesta dinnerware. The feast that Jenny had prepared over the past few days began to make its arrival. Following a thick, butternut squash soup, there was tender beef, ham, chicken, all kinds of potatoes, gravies, casserole vegetables, salad, biscuits and favorite desserts including raisin-stuffed creamy bread pudding (the twins' favorite).

After dinner there is lively talk of ghosts, goblins, jack-o-lanterns, costumes, parties, cider and doughnuts, then Tom suddenly saying, "What would you all say if I told you that Grandma Jenny is going back to school?"

Jenny gasped and everyone else in unison said: "WHAT?!" Even the twins who weren't quite sure of the particulars of the outburst, joined in, sensing that something remarkable had indeed happened. In rapid sequence there followed: "What for? Why? What course will you take? When will you go, days, nights? How can you go when you're babysitting for us?" Right about now, the twins, sensing this was not a happy occasion, began to cry, "Grandma, don't go away!!"

"Now, everyone, hold on here. Wait just a minute," Tom implores. "First of all, your darling grandma is not going away, not today or any day! And secondly, you all know how talented Grandma has been with her creative writing during the past years. She hasn't really had much of a chance to be serious about it because it was her choice to raise you and give you and the grandchildren her very best care. But now that you're settled with your family, well, you might say it's Grandma's turn, and I, for one, am very proud of her courage—for an old lady, that is!!"

"Daddy," Sally said while laughing, "that's terrible!"

The twins, seeing the laughter, started to loudly join in and pretty soon, either out of surprise or sadness or shock, everyone was in tears and/or roaring with laughter.

Testing the waters, Jenny meekly said, "Well, I suppose I could wait for another year before returning to school."

"No way, Mom. If you need to do this, then DO IT! Bill and Tom shouted, "Yes! It's Jenny's turn!" Tom raised his glass in a toast to Jenny:

"Here's to Grandma Jenny and winked at Jenny and she, in response, silently formed the words "Thank you" on her lips.

Aloud, Jenny happily exclaimed, "I love you all!"

Later, much later that night, as Tom held Jenny under the quilt of feathers and down, he whispered, "You know, Jen, no one in that undergraduate college will ever suspect that you're not the absolute newest, freshest, cutest freshman they've ever laid their cornbread eyes upon. You better watch out for all those college fellas, 'cause they just might see me waiting each night for class to end and offer this pretty young thing a ride home."

"Oh, they won't stand a chance, not with all the sweet talk in the world," Jenny responded. "'cause I know no one would ever love my 'put up' peaches half as much as you."

"And now...," Tom murmured, "no one will ever love your poem about 'put up' peaches more than me!"

THE HAT

Hats have a mind of their own. They don't care about others' comfort, and they will settle on the wearer's head wherever it suits them, or will swiftly make a quick departure on a sudden wind, whenever it pleases them. The perturbed owner usually chases the impudent hat, to no avail, looking quite foolish in pursuit, with knees bent high in an awkward sprint.

Hats are fickle. They hold no allegiance whatsoever to any one caretaker or owner. They love to fly about in the street, on a strong and furious wind, swirling up and cascading down and spinning in frenzied flurries, without sense or forethought and with utter disdain for any object in their uncharted path. By nature, a hat is flamboyant, impulsive, and will tease the owner with tantalizing coquettish behavior, as if to taunt and challenge capture and confinement, always beckoning but never embracing.

There ensues a game, between hat and owner similar to hide and seek, with frightening surprises and mystifying puzzling disappearances. The game concludes in gleeful and warm exchanges, but this time, suddenly, and without the slightest warning, the hat, on a sudden gust of wind, perhaps a March wind, crashed into a nearby most foul accumulation of a brackish collection of putrid waters, surrendering its once brilliant lavish felts, bows, and silk ties of rainbow colors and, in despair, lay helplessly, while desperately struggling, remembering pastel mornings of drifting clouds floating overhead in a tranquil azure sky. Inadvertently, its felt, velvet, and silks, once caressed by young maidens were unwillingly sucked into the murky waters and slowly and insidiously relinquished its once brilliant hues and fashionable design, rendering it fit only for a gutter urchin or a street walker or a horse's mangy head with holes torn out for ears. The hat had become worthless and full of shame. It once had pride and nobility and wore its thick feathers of envious purples, crimsons and majestic bronze in sprightly aplomb, daring the onlooker to stare to the point of impoliteness should the gaze remain too long, too lovingly, should bold admiration overtake one's better senses and too jealous in a need to confiscate, seclude and own.

The hat, longing for restoration and pride, struggles, at first seemingly in vain, with its limp and lifeless form. Then, beyond all measurement of anguish, it wills itself to grasp the wind encircling its brim and slowly begins to feel a warm breath of life embracing its sunken and misshapen form. Memories return of belonging and being tended and groomed, being briskly brushed and admired, and the hat, with great effort, begins to lift itself into the air remembering with each effort, what it was like to be free, without boundaries or limitations, and to join in warm companionship with a loving new wearer and vowing, this time, not to be tempted to ride a soft breeze, for there will always be a tempting soft breeze, sailing by...beckoning...

EMY

At age five or so, I was a sweet child, polite and imaginative. I am told I was well-behaved, bright and rarely the cause of any household disturbances. I had big, brown eyes, thick brown hair with bangs, which is short hair cut straight across the forehead. Being the youngest of three girls, I guess I was somewhat spoiled, which I couldn't see, of course, but my sisters certainly could. In fact, they would tease and chide me in a sing-song fashion: "Little Emy can do no wrong... Emy's Miss Perfect..."

Our family was neither wealthy nor poor. Like many others, we were surviving the tail-end of the Great Depression years. I remember very few toys, and on birthdays or Christmas, one present was all that any of us received.

I owned a large box of assorted, multi-colored and various-shaped buttons with which to amuse myself. My mother would often say, "Emy's such a good little girl. She's never a nuisance and can always amuse herself or keep busy." When I grew tired of sorting buttons, I played with my Raggedy Ann doll, a hand-me-down from my sisters, and some crayons.

I remember feeling quite happy with my life. I always knew I was my daddy's favorite, and I admit I enjoyed that privileged role. On second thought, maybe I wasn't, but it pleased me to think so.

Our house was on a small hill overlooking the Barge Canal. Barges would come by during the day, and when we heard them approaching we'd run to the edge of the hill and wave at the men below on the boats, and in return, they would wave back and sometimes sound a long, low blast from their horn. It was exciting because there was a feeling of connection with a world outside of our own and that maybe this barge would touch other distant shores.

I loved playing out of doors. We had a long stretch of lilac bushes and trees along the side of the house, and especially when they were in bloom, I'd take my doll and play beneath the flowering bushes. The scent was heavenly, and when I looked up at the sky, I would squint at the sun shimmering and sparkling through the lavender petals.

Our backyard had a swing, a see-saw and a sandbox, which we all used every good weather day we had. I loved our house and the yards, especially all the pansies and dandelions and the pond across the street that was edged with wild strawberry patches and filled with pollywogs. Sometimes we would mash the berries in a glass and have a fresh strawberry drink. I never ran out of something to do or things to play with.

We always had a lot of people at our house. One time, it was my oldest sister's birthday; she's eight years older than me, and we had a party for her. I noticed two really cute young boys sitting on the sofa in our living room. There was a small space between them that just fit me, and I sat down and looked up at them, batted my eyelids, and said, "Do you think I have pretty eye lashes?"

"Uh, yeah, sure kid, sure ya do."

I was thrilled and ran and told my mother. Of course, I told her that the boys just happened to compliment my lashes, and I, of course, did not seek the praise. That was such fun.

Usually, our day started with, "Come to the table; oatmeal's ready." My mother (I always called her "Mother") stayed home during the day with me.

"We'll be right there," my father usually replied, (He left the house every day to go to work) followed by my sisters saying, "Coming." After breakfast, they would go to school. I didn't, 'cause I was too little.

Lately, I had noticed my mother and father talking more, and sometimes they would whisper, and then one morning instead of my mother announcing that our cereal was ready, she shouted: "They're here!"

I had no idea what she meant and ran to the front door where she was standing. There, right in front of me, was a huge truck. When it stopped, several men got out and went directly to our furniture and started carrying all of it, piece by piece, out of the house!! They carried boxes with all our dishes, clothes, towels, everything! They took everything away!!! No one said anything to me except, "Come-on, Emy, don't get in the way; step aside; sit down over there…"

After the truck had left, everyone started cleaning up the mess, and I just walked around the empty rooms. I noticed a few of my crayons left behind, and I put them into my dress pocket. "At least, they can't get these," I thought.

When the cleaning was finished, my father said we were leaving, and I should get into the car. Instead, I hurried upstairs and waited silently in the hallway, not able to leave. How can I leave the only house I had ever known with the Barge Canal in back of our house, the swing and sandbox in the yard, the currant bushes, my secret hideaway in the lilac bushes…?

Everyone was now inside the car and they were calling for me to join them, blowing on the horn and gradually shouting louder and louder. I do not recall how and when I had planned my intended action, or if I had even planned it at all, but I put my hand into the pocket of my dress, wrapped my small fingers around a crayon and slowly withdrew a thick, heavy, greasy, black crayon. I felt confused and mad and with tears streaming down my face, I quietly and determinedly began drawing thick wide black marks on the walls in the hallway, narrow lines, broad wide lines, both horizontal and vertical, then circles and swirls in every direction, without a break, layer upon layer, executed harder and faster, while family voices continued calling my name. My oldest sister's voice was getting closer, and soon she was standing at the bottom of the staircase, urging me to join her, which I did.

"Emy, what have you been doing?" Didn't you hear us call you?"

I couldn't answer because my throat was choked up.

"Oh, Emy, you haven't been crying, have you? Everything's going to be all right, you'll see. You're going to love our new home."

"But I marked up the wall upstairs with my crayon 'cause I was scared and mad about leaving our house. I know I shouldn't have, but I didn't know what else to do," I replied.

Becky said she and Mom would probably come back to the house to clean it up and that she would talk to Mom and explain it all to her. Her guess was that I would not get punished because maybe it was not all my fault and just maybe the family, or all of us, were to blame. Oh, did that ever make me feel better, and I gave her a big hug. Becky is just about the most wonderful big sister in the whole world.

As I look back on those days, Becky would tell me that I was not an awful person because I got mad and scared, and she would teach me what else I could have done, like the use of three magic words: write, talk and walk. So instead of striking out, I could write about how I feel, or go outside and play or just walk around or talk about my feelings with someone I like. I was surprised when Becky told me that most other children even have imaginary friends they talk to or even have a monster under the bed or the closet who is to blame for all their wrong doing. If I had known that, then I could have named my monster "Mr. Mad" and put him under my bed and blamed him, but I know that's only playing and not real. Becky also said that when we're feeling mean, it's okay to ask ourselves why and kind of talk to our feelings, like getting to know them and then we're not so scared when they suddenly appear.

One time, I said, "Well, hello, Mr. Meany, what are you doing here today? Did you have something you want to say to me? What's that? I can't hear you very well. Well, if you can't speak any louder than that, why don't you just disappear and come back some other day? You say that's okay with you? Well, it's okay with me too! That felt good. I wasn't nasty or hurtful. I didn't throw anything or break anything or hit anything, and I'm not afraid of him. He's just old "Mr. Meany," and I've seen and talked to him before.

I forgot to mention, that if you don't have an imaginary friend or have a real friend to talk to when you need to, you can always use some of the ones that have been around for a while, like Santa Claus, or the Easter Bunny or the Blue Fairy or the Good Witch, and… any other you can think of.

I am told that when I was little, our house was located in an area where we were most susceptible to fierce thunder and lightning storms, and without fail, the most frightening ones occurred during the night time. Our family would get out of bed, go downstairs, my parents would unplug every electrical cord, and we would stand in a circle in the middle of the living room floor, away from any large windows, and there we would remain until the storm died down. Do I, today, have any queasiness about thunder and lightning storms? Of course! But do I get out of bed, unplug everything, and stand in the middle of the floor away from the windows? Certainly not! How can I when I've already buried myself under the protective layers of all of my blankets.

THE TAFFETA DRESS

Did it all start with the dress? The dress was so beautiful. The material was stiff, yet silky, and it shone in an iridescent sort of way, shimmering, catching the light, and when Ingrid took a step and then slightly swirled in a circle, it rustled and whispered, almost in a shy, yet bold sort of way. The colors were magnificent. There were blocks of lavender, pink, deep purple, turquoise and magenta, caressing and complementing one another.

Ever since her mother had bought the material, she would dream of when and how she would wear such a dress. Then Ingrid heard of the talent show at her school and, since she was studying the piano, she decided she would audition for the show, hoping that her mother would make a dress from the exquisite material for the occasion.

Ingrid had loved the piano as far back as she could remember. At age three or four, she would stand at her father's side while he sat at the piano and issued forth such beautiful music that she was spellbound watching his fingers glide across the keys, smiling down at her, loving her, while taking her to another world in the mystery of the sounds, so mesmerizing, so magical.

One day, she thought, I will play like that, I will, I know I will. She started lessons at an early age, six or seven, had studied with mostly neighborhood piano teachers and then, finally, was accepted at a well-known music school, at the preparatory level, intending one day to enter the advanced level of college studies.

Presently, at age 13, she was enjoying her new professor in the preparatory level, while attending the usual studies at the local high school.

Though she had studied for only a few years, performing at the piano, on stage, was not a new experience for Ingrid. The school she was attending had high standards of achievement, and in order to qualify as an honor student, a certain number of minutes of performing in recitals was required every year. Ever since Ingrid had begun her studies, she achieved the status of honor student every year. It was always a thrill to walk on stage, sit at the grand piano and share her musical abilities in a strange world of enchantment existing between herself and the audience. Once she started to play, it was almost a transformation, as though she was part performer and part listener. She could watch her fingers and still maintain a distance, immersed in the sounds.

Ingrid was known to some of her fellow students as a musician, for during part of her lunch hours at school, she would frequently play the piano, downstage, in the auditorium, and a small number of students would quietly assemble and listen to her. But the thought of playing on the grand piano, on stage, in front of hundreds of students was absolutely thrilling, and the thought of a new dress, which was, in itself an unusual happening, only added to the excitement. In addition, Ingrid told herself that since she was determined to become a concert pianist, the talent show at the high school would serve as a further useful experience.

Ingrid told her mother of the talent show and her intention to audition and pleaded for a special dress, made from that special material her mother had bought, should she be accepted in the show.

Her mother was concerned that Ingrid would not be able to keep up with her studies in the music school, so Ingrid told her she would learn a piece of music outside her usual curriculum and not let it interfere with her studies. Her mother did not care for the idea of Ingrid studying on her own without the benefit of her instructor, and reluctantly agreed. Ingrid was a little unsure if she could manage learning the new piece on her own, but concluded she had sufficient time and so set out, determined, in her endeavor.

Ingrid had chosen a piece of music, somewhat more difficult than her other music. The composition was *Claire de Lune* by Claude Debussy. Ingrid could play most of it, but had never studied the middle section, learning only the beginning and the ending, and on the day of the try-outs, Ingrid decided to audition, and should she be accepted, she would learn the rest of the piece before the day of the show. She realized she was taking a chance, but believed she could learn the entire piece.

On the day of the auditions, Ingrid crossed the stage towards the gleaming. black, grand piano, self-confident under the streams of light pouring down from the spotlights, challenging, even daring the admirer to come close, to sit down and touch its keys. Ingrid was not the least intimidated because of her experience at her school of music, and as she crossed the stage towards the gleaming piano, she visualized herself wearing her beautiful taffeta dress and being an outstanding success the night of the talent show.

She sat down, played what she had learned and memorized, and when she finished, the director requested that she meet with him at the stage apron. This particular director happened to be a graduate, an alumnus, of the music school Ingrid was attending.

"Ingrid, you have a very nice touch at the keyboard. However, the piece you have chosen is not exactly easy. Do you think you might have left out a portion of the music?" he inquired.

Ingrid, rather sheepishly replied, "I don't think so, but maybe I might have, I'll check it out."

"Hm-m-m, good, and who is your piano teacher?"

Ingrid told him and agreed to look for any missing sections of the music. To herself, she breathed a sigh of relief and was thankful to the director for his pleasant demeanor.

Ingrid was worried. She knew that she was taking a chance by telling her mother she would be able to perform the piece within the time allowed, but she so wanted that taffeta dress, and in particular, she wanted to wear it the night of the talent show. She diligently began an intense practice schedule and, without assistance from anyone, learned the entire piece, by memory. True, she was more sure of the parts she had learned earlier, but she believed she was ready for the performance of the entire piece. That night, after finishing her practicing, she went to bed early and lay quietly, looking at the taffeta dress hanging on the front door of her closet, catching the streams of moonlight—so appropriate for her selection of *Clair de Lune*.

Ingrid descended the stairs to the living room, feeling elegant and ever so grand. She could feel the thrill of nervousness and admitted to herself she was somewhat uneasy about the middle section of the piece, but she had practiced as much as she could and was ready to leave for the show.

"Oh, Ingrid, you look so beautiful," her mother exclaimed.

"Mother, you did it, you made it, and it's the most heavenly thing I've ever worn."

Finally, Ingrid is standing backstage in the auditorium, awaiting her turn, and when the Master of Ceremonies announced that she will play *Clair de Lune*, the audience let out an audible "Oh..." for the piece was well known and loved. Ingrid smiled and slowly and confidently walked across the stage and took her seat at the magnificent grand piano. Clearly, simply, her fingers took control of the keys, and she became part of the sounds lingering in the air, becoming somewhat mesmerized by the haunting, floating harmonies...then suddenly her heart stopped as she looked down at the keyboard and had no idea of where to place her left hand. In a time span of three seconds, she panicked, sucked in her breath and, as if nothing had happened, continued the piece, making up all the notes, yet keeping within the same key structure, tempo and mood of what she had already performed. Then, to her own astonishment, she once again, and with a slight smile of relief, resumed the piece as it was written and completed the composition, ending confidently with the part she knew so well.

The audience clapped enthusiastically as Ingrid approached the front of the stage and bowed appreciatively and was ever so thankful that she had survived her private shock of memory relapse. It was then she looked over at the director sitting in the front row of the auditorium, who smiled at her and knowingly winked an understanding nod that he knew what had happened and appreciated her ability to finish the music, though slightly flawed and unknown to the composer.

Ingrid returned the smile, silently said "Thank you" to him as she turned around in a graceful swirl, rustling the soft skirt of her dress to return to the back of the stage, and once again, bathed in the shimmering colors of her taffeta dress, she thought: "I guess I made some mistakes, in more ways than one, but I'll never forget this night, and I'll never forget this dress."

A WALK TO THE LIBRARY

I couldn't wait for the arrival of Saturday mornings. During this time of my life, (somewhere around early adolescence), I was engaging in and suffering from most of the earmarks of the typical stages of agony accompanied by self-consciousness, a little bit of shyness, with a touch of acting a la Sarah Bernhardt and Tallulah Bankhead, whenever drama was appropriate, which was often.

The excitement of Saturday began with the sound of a train emanating from our radio, the instrument responsible for much of our entertainment. The sound of the onrushing train signified the beginning of "Grand Central Station," an hour-long program of drama, comedy, tragedy and human interest stories, geared for all ages and delivered by famous actors on the wings of famous writers. Most of us were sure to secure a comfortable seat, shared the tray of sandwiches and lost ourselves in the drama coming over the airwaves.

The treasured event I just described marked the beginning of my precious Saturday and would have instilled enough warm feelings to last at least until midday. However, I had been given permission to walk to the library by myself on Saturday mornings for the purpose of exchanging my borrowed books for new stories of historical figures, new mysteries to be solved and new romances to be culminated in wedlock, having just attended, in mind at least, the marriage of "The Owl and the Pussycat."

I would collect the books I had borrowed the previous week, very carefully place them into a cloth sack with a shoulder strap so I could easily carry them, make sure I had my spending money and say goodbye to my parents and sisters. The walk to the library was probably just over a mile. My father would have driven me, but I declined his offer, for to set out on my own transfigured my little errand to a thrilling adventure, brimming with heart-throbbing heroes, adventures and mysteries.

I started my journey full of energy and with a spring to my step. I warned myself not to rush so I could enjoy the sights and the sounds as I clutched the cloth bag, feeling the books and remembering the princess in the castle who let down her long, golden hair and the handsome black-haired prince on a gallant steed (the books said things like "gallant steed" instead of brave horse) who rescued her. I believed that my rescue fantasy was similar to my adventure, though my destination was not a castle, but a library, which you must admit, looked something like a castle. I had once borrowed a book called "The Black Rose" about a handsome prince. I liked him so much I read it twice. I couldn't help but wonder, half-seriously, if I should need help, would I be rescued? This part of my walk always reminded me of fairy tales, because now the dull sidewalk and gray pavement of the road, transformed into a street divided by rows and rows of soft grasses, from which rose endless magnolia trees, dressed in white and pink blooms, holding hands for as far as you could see. Fragrant petals from the blossoms sailed about as if in a dream, and it took my breath away. Every week I joyfully anticipated the remarkable transition of the magnolias, as if they were intertwined with the stories and there midst the flowering trees I became the princess in the castle tower, waiting, somewhere between reality and fiction, experiencing both worlds. I was reminded of the jungle books, full of stories about perfumed flowers and strutting peacocks mysteriously cooing in rain forests as I allowed myself to dance with the plush fragrant flowers, gliding among the trees.

The next destination on my walk was the garden under the tree. As I approached it, I detected the heavy, pungent, sweet odor gradually becoming thicker and thicker, filling the air with drops of scented dew clinging to each bloom. The flowers lay under a centuries-old tree with huge swooping branches that first curled downwards before reaching up to the sky. The profusion of leaves left little space to admit the filtered sunlight, though it did seep in and silently scatter its dusty beams over the blanket of violets, myrtle and lilies of the valley. Whenever I arrived at the garden, I would stop and gaze and breathe in its scent and then listen, for I was not sure if they were Moon flowers. According to my book, Moon flowers sang each night, and if I waited, perhaps they might sing to me. But I needed to continue my walk, and they understood, as did the magnolias, now beckoning me to travel on.

I knew what lay ahead, and I thought of crossing the street to avoid passing by the house. It was not outright ugly or terrifying; it was morose, sullen and gloomy. It was a huge, four-story house, gothic in style and with fat thick pillars. In the center of the side of the house, were four gigantic panes of glass that looked into flights of stairs dimly lit with amber-colored lights having tones of costly rosewood and outlined by broad, sweeping banisters gleaming through the shadows. Above the windows was one high arch of glass that stretched across the width of the entire window, revealing more stairs that seemed to disappear into dark shadows. I didn't know if the house was haunted, or inhabited by spirits, or if ghosts floated over the stairs during the midnight hour. It looked cruel and menacing, and though it showed no signs of welcome, there was also a fascination with its very lure. In spite of having read some pretty unsettling tales by Edgar Allen Poe, famous ghost stories by well-known authors, and Nancy Drew's mysteries, this was the one place in my walk to the library where I did not linger. With one last look over my shoulder, I kept moving ahead, and soon I was able to pick out the granite building that housed the library.

The door of the library was heavy, and as I entered, I felt a little weary and enjoyed the cool, quiet air circling midst the books that almost seemed to say "Welcome. You made it. We've been waiting for you. Pick me, you'll like me," and on and on... Upon returning my books and presenting my card for the next week's selections, the librarian helped me select new stories, showed me some old classics, and we spent almost an hour browsing the collections. I told her about my delightful fantasies with the magnolias and the garden under the tree and the forbidding mansion with the dimly-lit staircase. She smiled, nodded and said she would expect to hear such tales from me, as she believed I had a fine sense of drama and imagination. She also suggested that one day I should write about my experiences. I thanked her for her loving ways and kind words, gave her a hug goodbye and started down the walk toward my home. I turned around to return her farewell wave (that's what books say instead of goodbye).

MY SISTER BEA

My sister Bea and I don't see each other very often; in fact, the last time that we did was around three years ago. She amazed me then, and she still does. She was born in Denmark and now lives in Sweden, which is only a tidbit of colorful information about her. The following is a brief essay about my sister Bea which will not be an in-depth study, but hopefully, a tender glance in my effort to portray her to the reader. I most likely feel the need to do this because she is modest, rarely speaks of her attributes, and I want her to know and remember my impressions of her. Too often, the kindest of people live their life without others truly knowing or appreciating them. Perhaps, now, that will not be the case for Bea.

Last week she informed me she thinks she will stop teaching Tai Chi for a while. She has been meeting with her group on those chilly Swedish mornings, floating through the air on their fluid motions in a quiet park, beckoning to the sun for a bit of warmth. Such a description of activity is only normal for her. To say she has kept active throughout the years is an obvious understatement. She has maintained a healthy lifestyle as well as a firm, decisive and positive frame of mind. If she doesn't know the answer she may be seeking, she will inquire until she finds it. Her desire to stay in constant motion was a family trait passed down from our father. As far back as this youngest child can remember, my sister and father were always going to or coming from. It was enough they enjoyed a weekly game of badminton, but to bicycle to and from the game as well? I was fascinated just to watch them. How old is she now? She's 81!!! And thriving!!! I'm 73 and praying!!!!

I first became aware of my big sister when I was three or four years old. She fulfilled many of the duties in caring for me and did so cheerfully and happily. She was responsible for bathing me, dressing me and similar daily routines. She would put me into one of those old-fashioned baby carriages, though quite in style then and referred to as a “baby buggy.” We must have resembled a child and her nanny in an old English pram, and we’d go for a walk; where, I‘m not sure, but I recall feeling the assurance of her presence. She was always comforting, with a head of deep, thick, brown hair, smiling through those big brown eyes.

One of her duties was to take me to tap dancing lessons, wait for me during the lesson and then take me home. I have no idea why she didn’t have a lesson, because as I know now, she would have liked to. But true to her nature, she was pleased for me. The dancing lessons culminated in a yearly recital held at a residence for senior citizens, commonly referred to as an “old folks’ home.” Our mother had sewn a blue taffeta dress with a white pinafore for me, and I, at age 4 or 5, in my patent-leather tap shoes, was taken on the bus by my sister Bea to the old folks’ home for the thrilling event. The recital went well, but I’m afraid to say that I gave my sister a bit of a hard time, as there was no way I was going to remove my makeup before I boarded the bus. I was convinced, at age 5, that I had embarked upon my future stardom. Of course, she gave in to my wishes and, as usual, made a fun time of the whole event.

Other events to recall, not in any special order: picking currants from the bushes in the backyard, one of our least favorite activities, leaving red stains on our fingers, which we had to scrub off with stiff bristled brushes; walking down to the banks of the Barge Canal and sitting on the edge of the hill, waiting for a barge to come by (what an event that was when one did thunder and rumble by, splashing torrents of water and almost drowning us in its wake! In the real world, it probably sounded its horn to us and stirred up a few little waves, but in the secret imaginative memory place of a five year old, we were lucky to escape the dreadful and powerful vessel); jumping, unannounced, into her bed during any time of scary dark night thunderstorms; always giggling and making fun of some adult family friends (in secret of course); and the best of giggles was at the family dinner table when some really cute young boys, who were the greatest of family friends, would tease us. One of those "really cute young boys" turned out to be her mate, her husband and father of their four children. My sister Bea was only 14, and the young boy from Denmark, was Helge.

I think I also fell in love with him because I never saw so much blond curly hair, such a winning smile, and the most gorgeous blue eyes—and besides that's what little girls are supposed to do. When I realized my affection was unrequited, I did not mind relinquishing my romance when I knew it was due to my sister. Anyway, she was 14, and he was 18, and they were soul mates for the rest of their lives, a relationship which drew to a close with Helge's death some 15 years ago.

Helge and several of the young men became U.S. citizens and enlisted in the armed services at the beginning of WWII. My limited vision of the war was enough to frighten me, which included sirens howling during air raids, black-out curtains, rationing of gas, oil, food, clothes, and the daily vigil kept by my parents for their families in Denmark. A number of my relatives worked with the Danish underground, and we were always fearful for their survival. In the U.S. everyone was doing their part for the war effort to help with the home front.

I recall my job. It was filled with romance similar to the Judy Garland and Deana Durbin movies of the era, as well as espionage, spying, covert operations and bribery. It involved the following plans: my dear sister was in high school and did not arrive at home until after the mail carrier ("mailman" in those days) had delivered the daily post, which afforded a certain member of our household ample time to sort the mail, find the light blue overseas envelope addressed to my sister from her sweetheart "somewhere in New Guinea," and carefully open it just to make sure that Bea was receiving properly censored mail. My sister Bea had decided the U.S. postal system was inadequate, so, our scheme of international spyworks, was that I, surreptitiously retrieve that mail as soon as it was delivered, slip it under Bea's pillow and pick up the quarter lying there in wait for me. I was delighted. My sister was delighted. Helge was delighted and, most likely, in some remote, unexplainable way, were the German and U.S. governments (who censored all mail).

The war ended. It ended all over the world, but never with more importance and celebration than when the buzzer on our phone system to the front office of Valley Court rang, Bea picked it up and said "hello", then in a shriek said "Helge!!!," dropped and broke the dish that she was drying, ran from the room and up the stairs to where her love was waiting. I could certainly guess, at age 10, why she, at age 18, seemed never to come back from the lobby.

Bea was Helgestruck. She was so entirely, overwhelmingly, entranced and in love with her love, that since then, when I was a witness to that encounter and later, the on-going relationship, I have always wished the same for every human being who ever contemplated a life together with someone.

It is not so much the events of living that transpired between us and still does, in spite of the distance between us, that I shall remember, but the constant, always there, reassuring kindness and love that she was and is capable of demonstrating throughout her life, not just to me, but to her love, her children and those close to her.

There is so much more to say. How can anyone go through a life and complain so little and yet accomplish such a wonder with herself, her little ones and husband? There are so many areas of her life to describe with affection, that should I attempt to begin, there would be no finish. Enough to say then, that I am delighted to have painted this portrait of a person whom I have admired and loved.

With continuing love and affection, for always, from Ellen, Bea's sister.

REFLECTIONS

This year, it was just the two of us celebrating Christmas Eve; quiet, no traveling north to see the kids, no dinner invitations—and it was nice. That's the best way to describe it: *nice*, not spectacular, just peaceful and calm. We played the radio station with the Christmas music and admired the brightly-lit trees in our front yard garden. We have two ten-feet-tall holly trees: full and bushy, on either side of the house, that we had strung with multicolored lights. One of the trees was close to our dining room dome-shaped double window and, when lit, at times you couldn't be sure if the tree was inside or outside of the house. I loved sitting in a semi-darkened room, listening to the music and gazing at the lights. To complete the Christmas Eve celebration, the scent of roasted goose slowly began to fill the air, just waiting to be accompanied by the fruit stuffing, sweet and sour red cabbage and little caramelized browned potatoes. We relished every bite of this traditional Scandinavian Christmas dinner, enjoyed sipping our coffee by the fireplace, and were soon snuggled under layers of down and good cheer.

When I awoke, it was still dark and the house was whisper quiet. My husband issued a muffled snortle when I inquired about his level of consciousness. Nothing startling there. But what followed was: I was wide-eyed, wide awake, and suddenly alert. I turned on my bedside lamp and discovered it was only 3:00 a.m. Why am I awake? What woke me? I got out of bed, put on a robe, and walked towards the bedroom door, once again questioning my husband's state of mind. His response was the same as before. But wait a minute. Why shouldn't I wake him? I don't want to go wandering around the house alone at this hour. On second thought, why disturb his rest? I switched off the light and walked out of the room into the darkened hallway. I was unsure of my exact destination, but continued on, so as to discover what I felt I should have known and what had prompted my unusual behavior.

The hallway led to the remaining rooms, all located on the first level. I slowly became accustomed to the darkness and made my way to the entrance door, went outside to our porch and plugged in the holly tree lights. As I stepped back into the house I sensed an almost mystic feeling in the silence. Just before closing the door, a soft whoosh of air breathed by my face and seemed to float and swirl, full of soft glowing lights of green, blue, red and yellow, now gently billowing up to the ceiling, gently cascading down and throughout the room in loops and circles, swirling, silent except for the whooshing sound sometimes passing close by and caressing my cheek. I noticed that the shiny black finish of the grand piano reflected the multicolored lights from the tree outside of the window, and the lights danced in response to the winds embrace of the branches. For a moment I felt as though I was in a school gymnasium during the prom and standing beneath a mirrored ball slowly turning overhead casting the images of color, floating slowly around the room. As I walked over to the piano, I sensed I was becoming immersed in the reflections, as if I had been written into a scene that was laid out in front of me, that I was a part of a drama, and the script was about to unfold. I carefully adjusted the position of the piano bench and slowly sat down at the keyboard, timidly at first, as though cautious about disturbing the opening stroke of the conductor's downbeat.

I started to play. I hardly looked at the keys, and would only glance at the position of my fingers every now and then. The music that poured forth from the instrument was mostly seasonal music, filling the room with the joy, mystery, celebration and wonder of the holidays mingling with the harmonies and melodies captured in the shimmering colored lights of the holly, reflecting upon the piano, upon me, and producing a majestic scene of oneness, of completeness, and as one entity derived from a composite of sound and light. Truly the music originated from the contact of my fingers with the keys, but with a strange feeling of detachment, as I watched them travel over the keyboard and I, becoming at once the producer of the music as well as the listener. I played every holiday song I had ever known or heard and used no written music, but glided effortlessly from one selection to another: some of old English origin, others of religious background, some from Mozart, from Bach, from more recent decades and even "White Christmas" plus a few current selections. I was astounded with my degree of accuracy in playing melodies I had never played before. I do not have perfect pitch, and it's impossible to acquire it. But I did significantly increase my level of accuracy. I played melodies, pieces, songs, hymns, carols, preludes, ballads, sonatas, a complete selection of music I had composed, fugues and some pieces chiefly for their chord combination, others of slower tempos, others that had a quick tempo requiring a more nimble touch, which I normally would have had following long periods of intense practice. Now, however, I was so surprised and delighted with my performance that I tested myself and repeated the fast tempo selection with similar success. As the music soared, so did my spirit. I was the capable and joyful performer as well as the pleased and appreciative audience. I arose from the keyboard, thrilled with my

Christmas Eve experience. Never, had I expected to perform again at such a level of achievement. I suddenly noticed my sleepiness and felt as though I had returned to a more normal, or different state. Shuffling tiredly along the corridor to our bedroom, I entered the room to discover my husband was now fully awake (of course, how could he have slept through my concert) and gratefully so, as he thanked me for the music that he had been enjoying for the past two hours. Two hours!! No wonder I was sleepy!

How do I explain the event? Was it sleep-walking, self-hypnosis, yoga, meditation or an out-of-body experience? Even though I tend to view these disciplines with great interest and believability, I cannot say that any one of them actually prompted the performance.

Perhaps my concert was simply part of an unexplainable mystery, a tale that belongs to Edgar Allen Poe or Stephen King, a tale for which there is no sensible cause-and-effect and only unexplainable happenings. There is no way to know for sure, or explain the reason.

I await an encore.

ABOUT THE AUTHOR

Ellen K. Williams

Having enjoyed success in the creative arts, as well as careers in music and psychotherapy, it was "the moving hand that writes" that led Ellen Williams to compose the enclosed verse, essays and short stories. Within a short period of time, she was published in several local papers, assigned a position as a staff writer and appeared in two on-line journals. Recently, one of the journals informed its readers: "Ellen Williams checks in with one of her trademark tongue-in-cheek contributions."

This collection exemplifies works of wit and humor, some outrageous and daring, some of serious intent and others that are tales of fantasy and imagination; all in all, a fun experience.

LaVergne, TN USA
17 September 2010
197487LV00005B/1/P